Sign Language
Athletes and Autographs

Phil Schaaf

MASTERS PRESS

A Division of Howard W. Sams & Co.

Published by Masters Press (a division of Howard W. Sams & Company)
2647 Waterfront Pkwy. E. Dr., Suite 300
Indianapolis, IN 46214

Printed in the United States of America

Library of Congress Cataloging-in-Publication-Data

Schaaf, Phil
    Sign language: athletes & autographs / Phil Schaaf.
        p.   cm.
    ISBN 1-57028-010-X
    1. Athletes--United States--Anecdotes. 2. Athletes--United States--Autographs.
    I. Title.
    GV697.A1S35   1994
    796'.092'2--dc20   94-36004
    [B]   CIP

Credits:

Cover design: Phil Velikan
Editor: Holly Kondras
Editorial assistance: Heather Seal, Terry Varvel, Marke Foutch, Kelli Ternet and Walt Stricker

INTRODUCTION

Every person that runs, kicks, hits or catches a ball dreams of excelling at the highest level. The applause, adulation and the self fulfillment from accomplishment are attractive lures.

Every athlete dreams of reaching the pinnacle. It's part of the motivation process. But, there is a price for success in the world of sports: media scrutiny, relentless attention from fans, unrealistic expectations from everyone, demands on maturity, etc.

The stakes in our multi-media society are enormous. In less than 24 hours, the whole world can be informed of circumstances in your life. It's not fair. The athlete has no control over the presentation of the information or the subjective interpretation by the public. Lastly, the public that can be so warm and receptive one day, can turn and vent its frustrations the next.

Imbedded in this skewed relationship is the need for the athlete to express him/herself. This book is really about that. It's about exchanges of emotions, feelings and attitudes between fans and athletes. For many fans, meeting an athlete and requesting an autograph is the defining moment of their relationship with a player. Unfortunately for the athlete, fans come at all times, and the celebrity must always be prepared to deal with his/her public.

Researching this book was an extraordinary opportunity to sample a diverse group of people. They come from all parts of society. Their candor, humor and humility is refreshing. Their time and thoughts appreciated.

Interviewing athletes is not always an easy thing to do. I have frequently told people that Cindy Crawford would have had much better luck in talking to some of the athletes than I did. Her sparkling eyes and dazzling smile would have probably elicited more interest than I did, but I have only great things to say about the athletes that I did interview.

These athletes did not owe me their time and attention, but they generously gave it.

People like Barry Sanders, Troy Aikman, Roger Clemens, Mark McGwire, Rick Sutcliffe, Dan Marino, John Elway, Davis Love III, Cal Ripken Jr., Ozzie Smith, Chris Mullin, Dave Winfield, Jay Novacek, Shaq, Luc Longley, Cecil Fielder, Chris Webber, Jason Kidd, Matt Biondi, Andre Dawson, Don Mattingly, Steve Garvey and Kristi Yamaguchi thoughtfully discussed their public. Every athlete I spoke with, including some who did not have entries in this book, took the time to talk with me and share their views on the autograph industry.

Before this project, I only owned one autographed item, a restaurant coaster that my brother had a celebrity autograph for me. However, I have worked with athletes in fund-raising and promotional capacities, and, through these experiences, I have seen how the public interacts with them. I believe that this book, which explores this relationship, will entertain sports fans of all ages.

I now own 141 more autographs and here are their stories. I hope that you enjoy them.

Photo Credits

Acknowledgments

This book really did rely upon the help, input and direction of many people.

Ted Walsh, Bronco Hinek, Dave Rahn, Michael Zagaris, Ray Tufts, Pat McPherson, Tony Fery, Bobby Monica, The Fabulous Bernie Brothers (D.I., Gary, Kevin & Stevorino), Lamont & Tenelli (92.3 KSJO) and Conner. Art Morley, Ray Fosse, Jay Alves, Mike Thalblum, Steve Vucinich and Bob Rose. Joyce Szymanski, Wilson Chan, Joe Hoffman, Julie Fie, Robert Harris, Bill Robertson, Rob Scicili, Leslie Ratay, Dave Trattner, Mike Williams, Cary Collins, Cheri White, Paul Haines, Luis Santo Domingo, Julie Marvel, Mike Hansen and Jeff Atkinson. Joe Carroll, Steve Brenner, Jared Franzreb, CGA, Malou Nubla, Andy Kuno, Patty Garrett, Roxanne Hasegawa, Patrick Toland, Beth Anderson, Ron Massa, Larry Carpenter and Steven Mitchell.

Ray & Jean Schaaf, R.J. & Janice Schaaf, Trey Schaaf, Chase Schaaf, Dave Schaaf, Sis Marquis, Tanjit, The Larson Family, The Ratay Family, D.A. Springings and Obersdorf.

Mel, Nick Zaharias, Michael Eagle Eye Zhurago del Ike Eisenstat, Laura Rice, Paul Hays, Sparta Gyro, Pete Keenan, Rob Simonds, Marcia Reeder, Adam Schor, Dwight Bandak, Hooker triplets, Clay Muster, Donna Lifsey and Mike "Blok" Gainza. Mike E. & Sooz Perkins/Big Al & Connie for key technology loan, including tech support. Lisa Larkin for software manipulation relief. Tool & OD for attempted *raparations*.

Tom Bast, Jon Glesing, Holly Kondras, Paul Mangiantini and Doug Glucroft.

The Mangiantini's, Thomas', Simonds, Barnes, Flaharty's, Gavin Christensen, Mallinckrodts', Doug Neil, Fernanda Jacintho Carapinha, Paul Hays, Mike & Tory Keady, Tom McInerny, Ramsey Masri, Damon Skyta, the Carthums, The Honda Hotel, The Shooters, Santo Domingo's, Zaharias', Larkins, Sweeneys, O'Donnells, Adairs, Schrigers, Owens', Cowans, Donnels, Youngs, Emmersons, Robbins, Habelts, Weidners, Shepards, Plumbs, Cox's, Fitchens, Polls, The Soz, La Familia de Fenosa, Pardini's, Petries, Hopkins', Morleys, Taylors, Jack Baker, Vardannis'. Hunters, Longstaffs, Vas's, Andy Kaffka, Hoovers, Micco's, Notti's, Brahney's, Kims, Connelly's, McCarthy's, Robbins', John Posthauer, Marilyn Lynch, Osgoods, Underwoods, Kings, Gainza's, Hafenrichters, Rich Risner, Nancy Lukas, Gene Bratcher, Jackie & Jerry Rice, Mike & Tona Wilson, and Linda at Team Powell.

Inspirational Icons

Beowulf, Pete Townshend, Copernicus, *Animal House*, Jimmy Buffett, *The Goat Brothers*, A dog named Road Trip, Jimi Hendrix, Duck Lake, Jack & Dan's (J.C., too), Brian Wachorst & his music, Jake Scott, Guillermo and The New Mecca restaurant, Mission City, The Peanut Farm, John Mellencamp, *Bear Territory*, Bruce Springsteen, Andechs, Full Sail Ale, Lake Shastina, Ultomato, Joe Louis, Lutz Long, Jackie Robinson, Dream Woman, *Mad Magazine*, Tommy's, Renault Espace, Tom Leonard & The Eliot Lounge, 21 Hews St., Saas Fee, The Road, La Boozeria, Noam Chamsky, Krems, The Public Library System & anybody or anything that has attempted to erode the world's ignorance base.

This book is dedicated to my Mom and Dad,
the two best roommates that I ever had

Table of Contents

Jim Abbott
NEW YORK YANKEES

A former Olympian from the University of Michigan, Jim began his career with the California Angels and was traded to the Yankees in 1993. He joined the elite fraternity of baseball's best by throwing a no-hitter in 1993. An inspired and inspiring player, Jim's persistence to pitch in the major leagues is a testament to hard work, effort and self belief.

When I was a kid, I was a big collector. I used to hang out at the park and try to get autographs. I even got Reggie Jackson's at Tiger Stadium. My Dad once brought home a Lou Brock autograph that meant a lot to me. Those things meant a lot to me then. They were a part of my own baseball dreams. Now, I think back upon how I felt when I was a kid, and I try to sign for people when I can. I try to make sure that I never turn my back on a kid and be as gracious as possible. But the autograph stuff can be a double edged sword. It seems to me that no matter how many people you sign for, you've still missed a few. If you sign 50 autographs, there are a group of 10 people upset that you couldn't sign for them. I enjoy giving autographs, but it seems the demand for them never ceases, and I feel bad when I can't sign for everybody. I do the best I can and try to get the people I missed the next time.

Troy Aikman
DALLAS COWBOYS

The first pick in the 1989 draft, Troy was slated to be the cornerstone to the Cowboys' return to glory. Four short years later, he steered Dallas to an impressive victory in Super Bowl XXVII where he was the game's MVP. He followed up in 1993 by leading the Cowboys to their second straight Super Bowl victory. A three-time Pro Bowler, Troy is the established leader of the Cowboys and one of the marquee athletes in America.

The one instance that means the most to me started with a sportscaster friend of mine a few years ago in Dallas. He asked me to go and visit this 10 year old boy in the hospital. The boy was a quarterback from a league in Texarkana. It turns out that the boy was driving somewhere with his father one day when the car broke down. The roads were pretty icy, and as the boy and his dad got out to see what was wrong with the car, another car skidded on the ice and ran over the boy. The child got caught up in the wheel well of the car, and by all rights, should have died. Somehow he survived. Unfortunately, he lost one of his legs and badly damaged the other one. There would be no more football for this 10 year old.

So, I went to pay him a visit one day, and when I got there, he told me that he was a Steve Walsh fan - who was our backup quarterback at the time. So he didn't even like me when I got there. But I sat down and spoke with him and his mom, and they were super people. I gave him my autograph and told him how brave he was. He really is a special kid, and we've stayed in touch since that time.

Athletes and Autographs

Sign Language

Sandy Alomar, Jr.
CLEVELAND INDIANS

One of baseball's best young catchers and the possessor of a rifle arm and powerful bat, Sandy was Rookie of the Year in 1990 and has already been an All-Star. Sandy is one of the tallest (6'5") catchers ever to play the position.

During my rookie year, I was driving home to my apartment and I noticed that a guy was following me. Every turn I made, every street that I went down, he was right there. I didn't know what was going on — maybe the guy was going to mug me. I was scared. I had no idea what he wanted, and I was new in town and didn't know my way around, or where the police station was located.

When I parked my car, I noticed that he had two little kids in the car and that confused me. I had no idea why a guy with kids would follow me. As I got out of the car, my heart was beating fast, and the guy approached me and asked for an autograph. I told him that the ballpark was the place to ask for autographs, not someone's driveway. But I signed for him and his kids. The park is the best place to sign. It's the place where fans and players celebrate baseball. When I have the time, I sign. The fans have been good to me. I like to give some effort back to them.

Morten Andersen
NEW ORLEANS SAINTS

The greatest contemporary kicker in football, Morten's accuracy and leg strength has been the most reliable constant in the Saints' gridiron success. He is their all-time leading scorer, and a perennial Pro Bowl selection. Morten holds the NFL record for the most 50+ yard field goals in a career (22). His booming kicks and clutch field goals will surely pave his way to Canton, Ohio and the Hall of Fame - a long way from his native Denmark.

I was at a mall, and these young kids came up to me on their bikes and asked if I would give them an autograph. I said, "Sure, what would you like me to sign?" Of course, I was expecting a hat, or card, but they told me they wanted me to sign their bike tires. That seemed rather strange, since their tires were black, just like my felt pen, but they insisted. So I signed their tires and they pedaled happily away. It just goes to show you that different things make different people happy.

Athletes and Autographs

Nick Anderson
ORLANDO MAGIC

The first draft pick in the history of the Magic franchise, Nick is also their all-time leading scorer. A smooth, high-scoring guard-forward, Nick is an established leader of the team both on and off the court. Nick, a Chicago native, starred at the University of Illinois. He wears number 25 in honor of his former high school teammate, the late Ben Wilson.

We were in Utah, coming out of the hotel on our way to the game, and this guy walks up to me and said, "Nick Anderson, give me your autograph. I'm handicapped, look at my sticker." This guy was older and dressed like Pee Wee Herman, and I just knew that he was lying. He kept saying; "I'm handicapped, I'm handicapped, sign your autograph." He kept shoving this sticker in my face to indicate that he was handicapped. But the fact that he was easily moving around, putting his hands in my face showed that he wasn't handicapped. So I didn't sign, because I thought that he was trying to trick me. When I walked away and got on the bus, he gave me the finger. I knew he wasn't handicapped.

Sign Language

B.J. Armstrong
CHICAGO BULLS

A former star at the University of Iowa, B.J. set the tone for his professional career with an unforgettable game against Nick Zaharias and his Gonzaga teammates in 1985. Since then, he has blossomed into an electrifying All-Star with the Bulls. Lightning fast off the dribble, B.J. is also an excellent three point shooter, and he led the NBA in trey percentage in 92-93. A community minded person, B.J. recorded a memorable TV commercial concerning the destructive forces of child abuse.

I don't take the autograph thing seriously. I never imagined that I would be here playing, much less the object of another's attention for an autograph. I can't understand why a simple signature is such a big deal when there are so many other important things going on. The whole scene seems fake to me. People see you on TV, and all of a sudden they believe that you are worth something. They think that you're something you're really not. Maybe that's just the way we treat our celebrities. People don't understand that we are just like everybody else. I sign, but I guess that I just don't always understand why.

Carlos Baerga
CLEVELAND INDIANS

Flat-out one of the best second basemen in the game, Carlos could also be considered one of baseball's true young superstars. He hit over .300 with more than 20 home runs and 100 RBI's in both 1992 and 1993. A flawless fielder with great range, Carlos is a true leader and impact player.

I was on the road, I think in Detroit, and the phone rings in my room at 7:00 AM. I answer it and I'm still asleep. The guy on the other end tells me that he wants my autograph. I told him that I was sleeping and to come back at 12:00 PM. I guess he didn't understand me, or thought that I was putting him on, because the next thing I know, he's knocking on my door. I opened the door and there he was with a card in his hand. I signed the card, closed the door and went back to sleep. After that I told the hotel operator not to forward any calls that early in the morning — unless it was an emergency.

Athletes and Autographs

Thurl Bailey
MINNESOTA TIMBERWOLVES

An effective swingman, Thurl has been one of the NBA's most consistent and effective sixth men during his career, averaging over 13 points and five boards per game. He is an offensive spark who also gives quality minutes on the defensive end of the floor. A key member of Jim Valvano's '83 NCAA Championship team, Thurl had a great view of Lorenzo Charles' game-winning shot.

Most autographs are exciting for kids, and it doesn't take much effort for me to sign my name on something, so it's always a thrill for me to make a kid happy. Most children have this special look of awe, and you know that the autograph moment is something that they won't forget. When I was a kid, I wasn't a real autograph seeker — mainly because I did not start playing basketball until I was older. I do remember getting Moses Malone's autograph at a Summer league. I know that Moses doesn't really sign for anyone, so I guess I was lucky. The craziest time was after we won the National Championship at NC State in '83. Those fans are passionate, and winning the championship the way we did unleashed a lot of emotion. All of the fans wanted to be around us, and we all wanted to be around them. It was a great time for everybody.

Sign Language

Charles Barkley
PHOENIX SUNS

A perennial All-Star, Charles is one of the most popular athletes in America, and probably the world. Charles is also a fabulous basketball player and a certain Hall of Fame selection. He has consistently ranked in the top ten players in both points and rebounds since he came into the league out of Auburn. Charles was recognized as the NBA's MVP after the 1992-93 season, his first season with the Suns. Charles also starred for America's first "Dream Team" and wowed the world with his broad-based talents.

This autograph stuff is getting out of hand, the industry is definitely too much. The emphasis has changed these days. It's now about money. It's not for the fun of it any more, and that's the sad thing about it. Now that autographs are being sold, we feed the animal every time that we sign.

As far as whether it means anything real to the person who gets the autograph— I don't know, because you just don't get to meet enough people. As many autographs as I've signed, I still haven't met one-half of one percent of the people in the world. In thinking that you're making a difference to the people you sign for, you've got to remember that everyone makes a difference. Some people good and some people bad. The key is to distinguish between the two.

But I collect some autographs. I'll collect an autograph of anyone who has made a success of themselves—not just other athletes.

Fred Barnett
PHILADELPHIA EAGLES

Fred is Randall Cunningham's favorite target in the Eagles' powerful aerial attack. A Pro Bowl wideout from Arkansas State, Fred missed most of the 1993 season with an injury, but recovered in time for the 1994 campaign.

I was signing for this one boy, and I had just started to write my first name. By the time I had finished the Fred part, the boy spotted Randall Cunningham and screamed; "There's Randall! There's Randall!" He snatched the program from my hand before I could start my last name, much less write down my number.

I waited for a moment to see if he'd make it back, but he never returned. Maybe Randall finished my name for me...."

Sign Language

Ed Belfour
CHICAGO BLACKHAWKS

A standout goaltender for the Blackhawks, Ed's tireless devotion to the game has brought him to the elite level of performance that few players can match. Ed was voted Rookie of the Year in 1991, as well as the winner of the Vezina Trophy, which is awarded to the NHL's best goalie. He holds the record for consecutive playoff game victories (11), and he has been an All-Star multiple times.

For me, signing autographs for fans is different, because I don't feel like I'm their idol. When I was a kid, I looked up to Tony Esposito and Bobby Hull as if they were super-human, and I can't believe that someone feels that way about me. I was seven or eight when Bobby Hull came to my hometown for an All-Star game, and after the game, we all crowded around him to get his autograph. He signed a special 50 goals in 50 games souvenir puck — which was a golden puck that I still have. I was so excited to get that autograph, and now, as a player, I just don't imagine that the fans feel that way about me.

I eventually told him that he signed my puck, and he said that he remembered coming to Carman, my hometown in Manitoba. I like to sign for little kids, because I was that little kid who met Bobby Hull. I make a point to push the adults out of the way to get to the kids. It's fun to sign for them. With adults, you don't know what they want your autograph for — a memento or money. The kids are going to take the autograph home and keep it forever, not sell it. It's humbling to think that these kids might look up to me the way I looked up to the heroes of my day. I feel like telling all of the business minded people who sell the cards to go away, because in their place could be a kid who wants to see what the player is like behind the uniform.

Matt Biondi
SWIMMING

One of history's greatest swimmers, Matt is one of America's most accomplished Olympians. He is best known for his remarkable 11 Olympic medals which he won in three separate competitions: one Gold in '84; five Golds, one Silver and one Bronze in '88; and two Golds and a Silver in 1992. Mark Spitz is the only other American to have won 11 medals in any type of Olympic competition. A graduate of UC Berkeley, Matt was also an All-American water polo player during his collegiate career.

I was in Carpinteria, which is near Santa Barbara, and I was getting a workout in when I noticed some kids watching me swim. At first there were just a few kids, but after 10 minutes, there was a group of almost 15 kids waiting at the end of my lane. So I got out of the pool, told my friend that I was going to sign autographs, take pictures and then be ready to leave. She said, "OK, I'll meet you in the parking lot when you're done."

So I was signing, talking to the group, and this one little girl in the group gets my autograph and then immediately runs away from the pool into the parking lot yelling; "I got his autograph! I got his autograph!" So my friend was out in the parking lot, and she asked the girl; "Who? Whose autograph did you get?" The little girl looked up at her and said, "I don't know." Even though she didn't know who I was— she got my autograph. And I think that tells you a little about what motivates kids to ask for autographs. In a lot of cases, they don't really know why they want it, just simply that they want it.

Best Wishes
Matt B___

Athletes and Autographs

18   *Sign Language*

Wade Boggs
NEW YORK YANKEES

With six batting titles and seven consecutive seasons with more than 200 hits in the 1980s, Wade Boggs' place as one of the greatest contemporary hitters is unquestioned. A nine time All-Star, Wade also has the highest average of any rookie in AL history (.349). Known as a player who rarely strikes out, Wade holds the AL record for most singles in a season (187). He has also led the majors in intentional walks a record eight times.

I had played a pretty bad game in Boston a few years back, and I wasn't in the most social mood when my wife came back towards the locker room to tell me that someone was waiting for me to come out to my autograph. I wasn't necessarily too eager, because someone always wants your autograph after a game. But this particular person turned out to be Jane Fonda. I was pretty impressed that a person of her stature would want my autograph. Knowing that someone like her had waited that long just to get my autograph cheered me up a little bit. She wasn't married to Ted Turner at the time, but a knowledgeable fan and a very nice person.

Chris Bosio
SEATTLE MARINERS

Chris is one of the most reliable and effective right-handers in the American League. Originally a Brewer, he signed with Seattle and instantly became a mainstay of the rotation. He threw a no-hitter against the Red Sox in 1993 and was rewarded with the AL Player of the Week award. A popular player with fans and teammates, Chris also serves as a member of America's Leukemia Society's National Sports Committee.

I was with the Brewers, and we were chasing Toronto ina pennant race. I'm stuck in post-game traffic on I-90. I was in a good mood though, because I had pitched a good game, we won, and it was a beautiful Wisconsin evening.

Traffic, meanwhile, is at a dead stop, and all of a sudden the door to my Jeep opens and this guy climbs in—right there on the highway. He recognized me and got out of his car and into mine.

"Great game, Bos," he says. "I was there. That was awesome. Way to go! Can I have your autograph?"

This guy was pumped up, and I'm stunned. I couldn't say anything. I'm just startled thinking to myself, "What's this guy doing here?" And before I know it, I'm driving down the highway with this complete stranger in my car.

"Look," I tell him, "I need to drop you off somewhere. I can't take you home with me."

Traffic has picked up at this time, and I'm driven about a mile with my passenger, and we were separated from the car that he had been in.

The guy was hilarious. "Can you just take me to my hotel?", he asks. "It's right up here."

The next thing I know, I'm dropping this guy off at a Holiday Inn, giving him an autograph. I drove off and never saw him again."

Sign Language

Rich Camarillo
HOUSTON OILERS

One of the NFL's best punters, Rich is a player who can kick for distance and accuracy. His ability to pin opponents deep in their territory with either a full or pooch kick is a valuable asset for the Oilers' defensive efforts. A career average of almost 43 yards per kick, Rich has been to five Pro Bowls and led his conference in net yardage statistics several times.

During my rookie season, I couldn't get used to signing autographs. The whole phenomenon of people wanting my signature blew my mind. I still find it hard to believe, because I know who, and what, I am— an ordinary guy who is lucky enough to play professional football. When I was a kid, I really idolized athletes, and it's hard to see me in their place now. But knowing that helps me understand the fans and appreciate their interests. I always try to sign for those who ask. I know what it's like to be a fan, because I've been there.

Joe Carter
TORONTO BLUE JAYS

A prodigious run producer, Joe is one of the most reliable power hitters in baseball. He is the only player in baseball history to have more than 100 RBI's for three separate teams in consecutive years. Joe is a three time All-Star and has had more than 30 home runs five separate times. He has also had more than 100 RBI's seven times. Blue Jay fans know that he is the first player in franchise history to hit a home run in a World Series game, but the world remembers his dramatic game winning round-tripper that he hit off Mitch Williams in the decisive sixth game of Toronto's second World Series championship in 1993.

There was this young boy, Sean, who was ill and staying at the Ronald McDonald House in Toronto. He was about 12 years old, and he was recovering from brain surgery. We became close after I visited him a few times. I invited him to a couple of games and brought him into the clubhouse to meet a few of the guys. I made sure to give him a bat, autographed baseball, hat and things like that. Twice he asked me to hit home runs for him, and both times I did. It's funny, because you say things like that, but you don't think about what you promised until after you've done it. It's like, "Oh yeah, I did promise Sean that I'd hit a home run for him." We were both excited that I could do it. It's not like Babe Ruth pointing, or anything like that, but it was nice to do. He's back in Bermuda right now, and doing really well. The people at the hospital said that he didn't smile that much, but that changed after we became friends. That's the best thing to hear.

Athletes and Autographs

Jose Canseco
TEXAS RANGERS

Stardom came early for Jose, winning the Rookie of the Year award in 1986 as a member of the Oakland A's. Two years later, he became baseball's first 40-40 player, with 40 stolen bases and home runs and was the unanimous MVP selection, only the ninth player ever to be selected in that fashion. A four time All-Star, Jose has twice hit three home runs in a single game and is one of baseball's most popular personalities.

I was in Kansas City, and late one night some guy was banging on my door, demanding an autograph. He banged and banged, made all sorts of noise and tried to break the door down. I called security, and they came and took him away. The guy was drunk, and he wanted my autograph. He didn't know that is definitely not the way to get my autograph.

The best autographs are for needy kids. I'm involved with Make A Wish, and when you're helping out in a good way and showing that you care, it makes the time well spent and worthwhile.

Sign Language

Chuck Cecil
ARIZONA CARDINALS

Undoubtedly one of the hardest hitters in the league, Chuck is also a fan favorite. Chuck, who was drafted by the Packers out of the University of Arizona, returned back to the Grand Canyon State as a high profile free agent in 1993.

My most memorable autograph was the first one that I signed. I've probably taken too many hits to the head to remember all of the others. But during my junior year at Arizona, some kids came up to me after a game and asked for my autograph. I almost refused solely for the reason that I couldn't believe that anyone would want it, or maybe it was a joke they were pulling on me. I asked them why they wanted it, and they shrugged and said, "Just because." That was a good enough reason for me, and I signed for them...I guess I'm not a tough negotiator.

Sign Language

Roger Clemens
BOSTON RED SOX

"The Rocket" has been the most dominant power pitcher in baseball from the moment he put on his Red Sox uniform. A three time Cy Young award winner, Roger has also led the AL in shutouts on four occasions, won the ERA title three times and led the league in strikeouts and wins twice each. Roger holds the major league record for strikeouts recorded in one game (20) and is the only player to have won the Cy Young award and MVP during the regular season, plus the All-Star game MVP. He did that in 1986. The heart and soul of the BoSox, Roger is one of the preeminent players in all of sports.

The best autograph moment, in terms of making both me and the recipient happy probably happened at the same time. I went to the Children's Hospital in Boston one day with some promotional leftovers. Whenever they have cap day or helmet day, I try to get some extras to take to the hospital with me to pass out to the kids.

This one particular day, I think that it was a Friday, I went to the hospital in the afternoon dressed in a golf shirt, jeans and boots. I went around passing out things and signing some autographs before I got to this one little girl's room. She was about 12 and had cancer. When I got to her room, her parents were there and they introduced me to her. She was a little antsy, and kept looking at me real carefully before she said to her mom, "That's not Roger Clemens. That's not the Rocket. That's not him." She really did not believe that I was Roger Clemens. She was so adamant that I decided to do something about it.

So I left the room, went back to the ballpark, changed into my uniform and headed back to the hospital. When I walked into her room, she flipped out. I gave her my autograph and she just about passed out. She was flabbergasted. Obviously to her, I look different in street clothes than as a ballplayer in a uniform. When she saw me in my Red Sox uniform, she realized that I was Roger Clemens the baseball player. Sure, it took some extra time, but it was worth it.

Todd Christensen
NBC

A former star tight end with the Raiders, Todd now toils in the broadcasting field as one of NBC's top game commentators. Known as one of the most loquacious (but not pedantic) announcers of any sport, Todd is also a frequent guest on Roy Firestone's Up Close program, where the two protagonists exchange witty and spontaneous persiflage.

I was in a mall and this lady comes up to me and asks me to personalize an autograph for her. "Of course," I obliged, "what is your name?" "My name," she said, "is LaDrenethia." "Uhh, excuse me," I asked, "could you please spell that?" So she did: L-a-D-r-e-n-e-t-h-i-a. I realize that there are a lot of different names out there, but this one definitely caught me by surprise. She was most likely the first and last LaDrenethia that I will meet and personalize an autograph for.

David Cone
KANSAS CITY ROYALS

Having more career strikeouts than hits allowed, David has been one of baseball's best pitchers for many years. He has excelled and starred for the Mets and Blue Jays before coming back to the Royals, his original team, in 1993. He finished 1993 among AL leaders in key statistics like strikeouts, innings pitched, and lowest opponent batting average. A durable player, David had one of the highest winning percentages in NL history in 1988 when he finished 20-3 (.870) for the Mets. David also won the Cy Young award for his sterling performance (16-5, 2.94) in the strike-shortened 1994 season. A native of Kansas City, he is an All-Star player and true local hero.

When I was playing for New York, I went to a Bar Mitzvah as a celebrity guest and there were kids everywhere having a great time. The mother of the boy who was having the party had a memorable request. She was going to pop out of the cake at the time it was brought down into the party, and when she did, she wanted me to come over and sign her left breast with a ball point pen. Her husband, meanwhile, was going to videotape the whole thing. Sure enough, the music came on, the cake came out and the mom popped out just as planned. I walked over, signed the top of her breast, and the kids went nuts. She wasn't topless or anything like that. The kids loved it, and somewhere the whole thing is on videotape.

Brad Daugherty
CLEVELAND CAVALIERS

The first pick in the 1986 draft, Brad is yet another perennial All-Star from the University of North Carolina. Brad averages a 20 points per game and pulls down an excess of 10 rebounds each game as well. A deft passer and agile defender, Brad's unselfish and hustling play is the key to the Cavs' consistent success. He is also the leading rebounder in the Cavs' history.

I was bass fishing on a lake in Florida called Farm 13, and this guy sees me. He whips his boat around and starts to chase me. He waved me down and I asked him what he wanted. He asked for an autograph and I gladly gave him one.

Sign Language

Andre Dawson
BOSTON RED SOX

Known as the "Hawk," Andre is a future Hall-of-Famer whose greatness has spanned three All-Star decades. Andre, originally an Expo, starred for many years with the Cubs before signing with Boston. Despite 10 knee operations, he has accumulated over 2,700 hits, 400 home runs and 1,500 RBI's in his 19 seasons in the major leagues. The National League MVP in 1989, Andre has won numerous Gold Gloves and team awards over the course of his great career. A true gentleman of the game, Andre's exemplary play will forever inspire fans.

I was at a card show once, and a woman gave me a pair of panties to sign. She told me that she wasn't going to wear them, she just wanted me to sign them. I refused to sign them — even if she wasn't going to wear them.

Another time, a woman asked me to sign her shirt for her, right next to her chest— while she was wearing it.

Again, I refused. It seems that I have a "no personals" policy when I sign autographs. In both cases, though, they each had a photo, and I willingly signed them. So they each got their autographs— just not where they wanted them.

Todd Day
MILWAUKEE BUCKS

The eighth pick in the 1992 draft, Todd is a multi-dimensional star for the young Bucks. He is the franchise's first ever lottery pick, and as an All-American at Arkansas, he had the game to warrant the honor. Todd can score, rebound, defend and lead the break, and as a rookie, even had a rare four point play against the Heat. A hard-working basketball "junkie," Todd also plays in summer leagues with some of his fellow Bucks.

In college, I heard about this child who was in the hospital with cancer. He had a Todd Day jersey. I went to the hospital, met him and signed his jersey and got to know him. He was about 11 years old, and it was real sad to think about his struggle for life. Things weren't looking too good for him, but he pulled through and is now living a normal life. I still see him when I go back to visit, and it's a reminder of the most special autograph that I have signed.

Sign Language

Chris Doleman
ATLANTA FALCONS

A ten year veteran from Pitt, Chris has been one of the NFL's most dominating defensive lineman since he came into the league. He has been the NFC's sack leader twice, and voted to play in almost every Pro Bowl. Originally a Viking, Chris went to Atlanta to help Pierce Holt form one of the best D-lines in the league. Chris has also returned a fumble for a touchdown — a rare feat for a lineman.

A lady asked me to sign a shirt "Happy Birthday Stan." I don't know what came over me, but I ended up writing "Happy Birthday Stand." I immediately realized what I had done, and I tried to fix the situation and cross out the "d" at the end of the word. But instead, I ended up scribbling all over the shirt and made a big mess. I looked up at the lady, apologized and offered her 20 dollars to buy a new shirt. She refused the money, but the guy who sold her the original shirt gave her a free one, and I got it right the second time.

Joe Meets his Match

In 1976, my brother Dave (age 11) announced to the family that he was going to have lunch with Joe DiMaggio. A friend's father knew the Yankee Clipper, and he was going to arrange a luncheon. At the time, the true meaning was lost upon me and my two brothers. We knew that Joe D. was a hero, a fabulous ballplayer and all, but we did not understand the true significance of his career beyond his Mr. Coffee commercials. The three of us began to sense that it was an enormous privilege, however, because every adult that heard of Dave's luncheon plans was genuinely impressed.

When Dave left, he asked me if I wanted to ask Mr. DiMaggio anything. "Sure," I said, seizing the opportunity, "ask him for his autograph." Dave said that he would try his best to accommodate my request, and that he'd be home in a few hours.

The group met, and Dave, a shy youngster, quietly ordered a cheeseburger and fries. Lighthearted conversation filled the time and by the time Dave's cheeseburger got in front of him, he was hungry.

Dave liked his cheeseburger and fries with lots of beautiful, red Heinz 57, and that's where the trouble started. Because before he could start eating, Dave needed to get his condiments situation straightened out.

Meanwhile, Joe is to Dave's left, and nattily attired in a white suit. He pays absolutely no attention to Dave's processed tomato needs, and starts into his own lunch. That might have been a mistake, because if he looked to his left, he would have noticed that little Dave was hitting his bottle over and over, trying to get that ketchup trickle started in order to finally start eating his burger and fries.

"Thwap," sounded the hand and bottle collision.

"Thwap." He hit it again.

"Thwap, thwap, thwap, thwap, thwap, thwap, splatttt."

The ketchup finally came out of the bottle. The only problem was that it didn't land on the burger. It landed all over Joe DiMaggio.

Dave was horrified. He couldn't believe that the ketchup landed all over Joe. He could barely speak, he was so shocked and remorseful.

DiMaggio, of course, brushed it off with great graciousness. He felt badly that this little boy felt so guilty, and he did his best to assuage Dave's shame. Dave meekly ate his lunch, apologized yet another time to the Hall-of-Famer, and said goodbye.

But he had one last question before Joe left:

"Mr. DiMaggio, my brother Phil would like your autograph, could you please give him one?" DiMaggio's response is pictured below. It was the only autographed anything I owned before research on this book started.

Mark Eaton
UTAH JAZZ

A long time starter for the Jazz, Mark was quietly one of the game's greatest defensive players. In fact, he retired as the NBA's second career shot-blocking leader— only behind Kareem Abdul-Jabbar. Furthermore, he consistently was placed on the NBA's All-Defensive teams during his productive career. In 1984-85, Mark set the NBA record for blocks in a season (456), and per game (5.56). A graduate of UCLA, Mark was a league All-Star in 1989.

One thing sticks out in my mind isn't necessarily an autograph story, but it's along the same lines. There was a sick boy in the hospital, and he was in pretty bad shape. He was a fan of mine, and I gave him a pair of my shoes to hopefully inspire him a little. He really liked the shoes, but they couldn't help him recover from his illness. When he died, they brought my shoes to the funeral— as a small part of the ceremony.

Blue Edwards
BOSTON CELTICS

An explosive guard from East Carolina, Blue expects to bring his offensive prowess with him to the hallowed Celtic tradition. Blue, an effective shooter and open court guard, joins new teammates Pervis Ellison and Dominique Wilkins to lead Red Auerbachs' troops down the parquet towards another championship.

I was with Utah and we had a stretch of three days in LA. We were staying in Marina Del Rey and there was an older guy who knew we were in town, and he was always waiting for us in the hotel lobby with stacks and stacks of all our cards. We all signed for him. He was very persistent and always there, no matter what time we got in. He kept coming back at different times each day until we noticed that it was not a coincidence that he was there. So we started to duck him. We'd go out the back door, through the kitchen— anything to avoid this guy. But he figured out what we were up to and he started to wait for us behind cars, bushes, everywhere. He'd pop up like a Jack in the Box when you'd least expect it. He was busy sneaking around while we were sneaking around. By trying to get so many autographs, he messed it up for him-self. At first, everyone signed for him. But word quickly spread around because the whole team got tired of his act and we decided that we wouldn't give him any autographs. None at all— we were going to shut him down. But he was relentless, and wouldn't leave us alone. He showed up everywhere. Finally, we had to talk to a security representative, and they ran him off. But then he parked across the street in a restaurant and still came after us. Most guys that ask you for an autograph, you never see again. But this guy was around for three days. It must have been financially motivated, otherwise I can't imagine why anyone would want to spend that kind of time looking for autographs. I haven't seen him since, but I'm sure he's still around. I don't miss him at all.

Sign Language

Mike Eruzione
USA HOCKEY

Mike was the team captain of the underdog 1980 Olympic Hockey team that surprised the world by winning the gold medal at the Lake Placid Olympics. A defenseman, his leadership and gritty play was instrumental in beating teams like Finland and the Soviet Union. Waving his teammates to the victory stand during the jubilant medal ceremony, Mike and his teammates emphatically answered Al Michael's rhetorical question: "Do you believe in miracles?"

Right after the 1980 Olympics, this girl walks up to me and told me that she had a $50 bet with her boss that I would sign her chest. I didn't take her seriously until she dropped her shirt, and showed enough of herself to win the bet. I wrote, "Mike Eruzione was not here," and left her to collect her winnings on her own. I still get a lot of mail, especially since the hockey cards have come out. I get about five to ten requests a week from fans all over the country, and from Europe as well.

Sign Language

John Elway
DENVER BRONCOS

A rifle armed superstar, John has led the Broncos to more comeback victories than any other player in the history of football. John has thrown for almost 35,000 yards and 200 touchdowns in his ten seasons with the Broncos. A four time Pro Bowl player, two time All-Pro selection and former collegiate All-American, John's greatness can be traced all the way back to Granada Hills High where he shared co-athlete of the year (1979) honors with middle distance runner Farron Fields. His trademark two minute drills are a thing of beauty— to everyone but his opponents. The most prolific passer in Bronco history, John is a certain Hall of Fame inductee when his career closes.

I don't mind signing autographs, I just don't want to be abused by the collectors who are in it for the money. I like to sign one for a fan, but if someone has a stack of ten pictures, two helmets and three footballs, then I think that something is up. I always personalize pictures and cards, and try to not contribute to someone's business— because they sell to the legitimate fans who want to meet you and get your autograph for their collections.

Boomer Esiason
NEW YORK JETS

Boomer has been one of the AFC's best and most productive quarterbacks. Originally drafted by Cincinnati, he made the "no huddle" offense a threat on the way to Super Bowl XXIII. Boomer has already thrown for 30,000 yards and 200 touchdowns in his illustrious career. A four time Pro Bowler and Sporting News' Player of the Year in 1988, Boomer came to the Jets in 1993 in the hopes of bringing them another Super Bowl bid.

As a kid growing up, I never thought that I'd be signing anything but checks to pay bills. Now, I sign everything imaginable that a fan can bring me. It always seems strange that anyone would want an undergarment signed, but they bring them to you. That would seem to be the last place you'd want an autograph. Here's the athlete where you least expect him. Some people even ask me to sign "Norman," my real name, and I sign that for them.

Brett Favre
GREEN BAY PACKERS

A rifle-armed, two-time Pro Bowler, Brett's presence and play has brought renewed hopes to Titletown, USA. Brett was traded by the Falcons for a first round draft pick and stepped into the Packer's lineup to immediately produce for Mike Holmgren's sophisticated offense. Brett loves the deep passing game and will linger as long as possible in the pocket for his receivers to get open. A native of Mississippi, Brett spends his off-seasons there.

I've only been in the league for a while, but I am shocked at the things people ask you to sign. I've signed what seems to be entire merchandise catalogs: posters, hats, shirts, cards, jackets, sweatshirts, footballs and even golf balls. But the requests don't stop there. Those are only the routine items. It gets interesting when they start asking you to sign limbs and other parts of the body. I always think they'll regret having their arm signed when they try to soap it off in the shower. I always sign everything asked of me, except certain parts of the anatomy which I refuse both to mention and sign.

Sign Language

Cecil Fielder
DETROIT TIGERS

The premier power hitter in the majors, Cecil is one of only 11 players in the history of the game to have hit more than 50 home runs in a single season. He is the second player in ML history to have led the league in RBI's three consecutive years, and the first player to have hit a ball entirely out of County Stadium in Milwaukee. Originally a Blue Jay, Cecil starred for the Hanshin Tigers in Japan's Central League and was among that league's offensive leaders in all major categories. Cecil returned to Japan in 1992 with a barnstorming team of All-Stars on a goodwill tour.

As far as special cases of meeting people in hospitals —that is not necessarily for the public to know about. I have several personal relationships like that, and I want to keep them that way.

Having played in both the US and Japan, I've seen all forms of requests, from all types of people, and the one constant is that you get a lot of requests. I'm always amazed at how kids ask me. "Hey, you," is not my name, and I wonder where they learned to talk like that. If I heard one of my children speak like that, it would be an opportunity to teach a lesson. I demand that people be polite. That's my only rule. The kids in Japan were all so polite. They had a genuine feeling about them, and it really stood out, because it was consistent. The difference between here and there is noticeable. If a kid admires you, why shouldn't they be courteous? Kids like that probably aren't respecting each other, and those guys are missing out.

When I was young, I met Nate Colbert, who was a star for the Padres. My step-grandmother was his aunt, and she arranged for me to meet him at Dodger Stadium. When I met him, I shook his hand and talked to him and didn't even think of getting his autograph. Nowadays, a kid approaches you with something in his hand rather than having it extended for you to shake, and I wonder why that is. The players see the people that work at it every day, and when we see the same faces, we realize that the autograph thing is too much, because it shows that some people spend all of their time getting signatures rather than going to school or working. And that means that the fans who really want them are not getting them.

Julio Franco
CHICAGO WHITE SOX

Julio is a former batting champion and clutch RBI specialist, as well as one of the AL's most consistent right-handed hitting stars. A career .300 hitter, the Dominican Republic native has fought through tough knee injuries to still be one of the toughest outs in the American League. Originally a second baseman with Texas, Julio is primarily a designated hitter for the White Sox.

There was a guy in Milwaukee who had wanted my autograph for a long time, like six or seven years. For some reason he could not get it. Finally, he met me, got on his knees and begged me to sign. After I signed, he started to cry and even hugged me. "God bless you," he said to me. He had been following me for years, and it meant a lot to meet me. But it also touched me that something like that could mean so much to someone else. It made me emotional. He got down on his knees in public, unashamed of being so open about how he felt. He wasn't a collector, but he had been following me for years and just wanted my autograph.

Mike Fratello
CLEVELAND CAVALIERS

The former head coach of the Atlanta Hawks and former "Czar of the Telestrator" at NBC, Mike is now the man bringing a new direction to the Cavaliers franchise. An excellent communicator and motivator, he is one of the marquee coaches in the NBA.

As a coach, you feel like a movie director. You help stars do their thing, and try to create the best possible situations for them to excel. When that happens, you achieve an unbelievable level of satisfaction. As a coach or announcer, you tend to get a lot of publicity, but again, like the movie director, not as much as the players. And that's the way it should be. Therefore, whenever a child approaches me for an autograph, I feel that there is a slight chance that it will be for a request for a locker room pass to meet the guys. It's important to use your position to help people when appropriate. Whether someone wants my autograph, or that of a player, I try to be receptive. So far, however, no one has asked me to get them Marv Albert's autograph.

Steve Garvey
BASEBALL

A member of the longest running starting infield in baseball (Garvey, Lopes, Russell and Cey), Steve personified the great Dodger teams of the 1970s. He played in more than 1,200 consecutive games in his career, fourth on the all-time list, and was an All-Star multiple times. He led the NL in hits twice, and was the 1974 MVP. Steve left the game with almost 2,600 hits, over 1,308 RBI's and the best fielding percentage for a first baseman (tied with Mattingly and Parker at .995) A clutch hitter, he hit the most memorable home run in franchise history when his round-tripper against the Cubs brought San Diego's only pennant in team history.

There are so many different instances (that I've signed autographs) and the ones that stick out are the times I seized the initiative to go to them. If there is a large group around me and I went into the crowd and picked up the little kid who is too small or too shy to ask for himself, that's neat to do.

It's not so much the idea of simply signing my name. It's a chance to share something with the fans. It's a real important relationship that I have always enjoyed, because it's both easy and rewarding for both myself and the people that I'm lucky enough to meet. I try to be sensitive to the people I meet, and that moment of communication is always worth the time.

I was lucky, because my dad worked for the Dodgers and that gave me access to some pretty special people. My first autographed souvenir was a team ball signed by the 1956 World Champion Brooklyn Dodgers, and that was truly a big deal. Not too many kids on the block had one of those. I got Mickey Mantle's autograph and Yogi Berra's when my dad drove for them a few times and even after I became a player, those were moments I always remembered.

Horace Grant
ORLANDO MAGIC

A tireless rebounder and defender, Horace has forged a reputation for subordinating some of his awesome talents for the good of the team. His sacrificial play, in fact, was one of the main ingredients to the Bulls' three straight NBA titles. A star at Clemson, Horace became the first player in ACC history to lead the conference in scoring, rebounding and shooting percentage. He brought this stability to the Magic as a high profile free agent signee hoping to add to his championship resume. Not only is he the most famous person to wear goggles, Horace and his identical twin brother, Harvey, (Washington Bullets), are the two most productive siblings playing in the NBA today.

Someone brought my brother's jersey up to me and asked; "Harvey, could you please sign your jersey?" So I signed Harvey's name and the person went away very happy. It was a clean transaction. In signing autographs, I like the little kids — they give me a genuinely good feeling.

Sign Language

Juan Gonzalez
TEXAS RANGERS

The AL's home run champion for 1992 and 1993, Juan is also one of the game's best all-around players. His power is self evident, but his fielding and clutch hitting have been major contributors to the Rangers ascension to the top of the AL West as well. The 1993 season was a great one for this young star, as he tied Barry Bonds for the major-league lead in homers and led the Rangers in home runs (46), RBI's (118), average (.311), slugging percentage (.632) and total bases. A native of Puerto Rico, where he is known as "Igor," Juan devotes a lot of resources and time in community activities. Currently teamed with Jose Canseco and Will Clark to form a new "Murderer's Row," Juan hopes to hit more home runs for his loyal fans.

Autographs are not as important as the message you can bring to people. Back home, I talk to a lot of people, mainly kids. It's important to talk about drugs, going to school, the future. Little kids in my country look up to ballplayers, and it's important that I show them that I'm human, that I care, that I feel what they feel. I love kids, all people, and I talk to them, try to teach that whether it's sports, or the law, or becoming a doctor, they can change their lives by trying hard. Especially at home, in the bar-rio, I talk and tell the kids to dream, to have a great atti-tude, and to think big. I tell them that I live a dream, and I try to bring my dream to the fans. Sometimes by signing an autograph, I do that for them. By sharing with them, it shows that I care. We are all human — and all the same. I try to give them a good message, because this world is crazy with all of the drugs and violence. I try to make a difference for the little ones — they're so innocent — God bless them all.

Ron Harper
CHICAGO BULLS

A star with both the Cavaliers and Clippers, Ron has been one of the most electrifying players in the NBA since coming out of Miami of Ohio. A former All-Star, Ron can score off the fast break, and in the half court offensive set. He's also a sneaky defender and routinely ranks among the league leaders in that category. Perhaps Ron's greatest accomplishment is that he fought back from a debilitating knee injury to regain his status as an elite player.

There are a couple of different types (of autographs). I enjoy going to a hospital and making little kids happy. The ones that I don't enjoy are when I get recognized at a night club, or someplace where I'm trying not to be the basketball player that people recognize.

One situation that I like is when a few kids will see you, and one of them knows who you are. He'll try to convince his friends that you are somebody. The kid will whisper, "That's Ron Harper. He's a basketball player."

Then his friend will say, "Aw, you don't know him." Finally, they always seem to get enough courage to come up and ask who you are, and if they can have your autograph.

I really like the shy kids. They have a scared look like, "I really don't want to bother you, but I'm going to ask you for your autograph anyway." They always make me laugh and always get my autograph.

Thomas Hearns
BOXING

More popularly known as the "Hit Man," Tommy is one of the greatest ring gladiators of any era. Having won five different titles in his career, Tommy's epic battles against Sugar Ray Leonard, Roberto Duran and Marvin Hagler are some of boxing's most historic matches. Of his 51 victories 41 came by knockout, most from his thundering right hand. He has earned millions from his ring career. But more importantly, he was won respect from his peers and adoration from boxing fans around the globe.

The most important autographs are with the kids and the people who sincerely want to meet you. The children that look up to athletes appreciate it when you can spend some time with them. The autograph is proof that they met you and shared something with you. When you spend time with people, you're enhancing the image of yourself, your sport and all athletes, because you're giving people contact with a performer. The fans are what make you—it's an easy decision to give something back to them.

Rickey Henderson
OAKLAND ATHLETICS

Baseball's all-time stolen base leader, Rickey is undoubtedly the game's greatest lead-off hitter. Not only is Rickey the career stolen base leader (over 1,000), Rickey holds the single season record with 130. He also holds the club record for both the A's and Yankees for base thefts. The AL's MVP in 1990, Rickey was the playoff MVP the same year. Rickey also holds the MLB record for leading off games with a home run, (66 and counting). An Oakland native, Rickey is a certain Hall-of-Famer.

When I was a kid growing up (in Oakland), I tried to get Reggie Jackson's autograph a bunch of times— at least ten. Every time, he'd say "Tomorrow, tomorrow," or "Not right now, I've got to go to batting practice" or whatever. The only way I could get his autograph was to become a major-league player— and only then did I finally get it.

I like my relationship with the fans. They make the game fun to play, and it's nice to wave, sign, or just chat with them. When I walk away from the game, I'll have a lot of memories of some great people who made the game worth playing. They'll never leave my mind or heart.

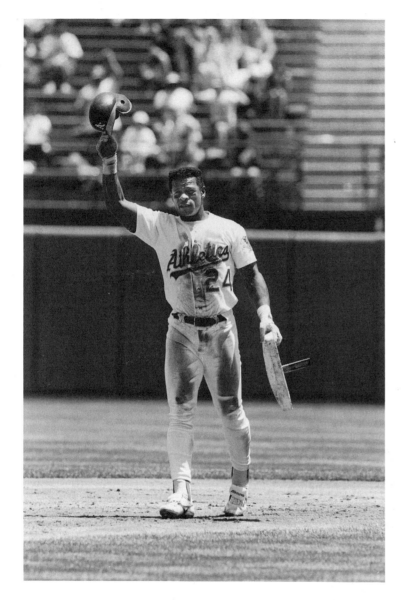

Athletes and Autographs

Joel Hilgenberg
NEW ORLEANS SAINTS

One-half of the only sibling center tandem in the history of the NFL (the other half is his brother, Jay), Joel Hilgenberg is one of the league's best centers. He is an excellent long snapper as well as being effective in both run and pass blocking formations. A native of Iowa, Joel attended the University of Iowa before being drafted by the Saints. Not known as a downfield threat, Joel caught a nine yard pass in 1990, a lineman's dream.

One thing that I know has changed is my signature. It used to be that you could identify every letter in my name. Now it's gotten to the point where it's loop-loop-loop, and that's all folks.

The most important autograph sessions are the ones at the Children's Hospital in New Orleans. We go there with hats, pennants, shirts and things to try to brighten up their day. I'd even stand on my head if I thought it would help them. The kids really light up when they see us, and it means a lot to us to see their excitement. As a player, you know about pain but not the kind of pain that they're in. At the very least, we try to take their minds off the suffering that is a constant part of their daily lives. If we can be a small dose of medicine, then a smile is all we need to know that we're doing a little something as football players beyond simply entertaining fans.

Pierce Holt
ATLANTA FALCONS

One of the NFL's best interior linemen, Pierce came to stardom the hard way. He worked out of high school and decided to give football a try and landed a scholarship at Angelo State. He starred there and was drafted by the San Francisco 49ers where he became a dominating presence on the line of scrimmage. A free agent signee of the Falcons, Pierce brought his hard-nosed, relentless pressure style to the Georgia Dome. A true gentleman, Pierce is an inspirational player and person.

The most memorable request for my autograph was the first, because there was no way to have expected it. I was at the Senior Bowl, and all of a sudden this girl comes up to me and asks me to sign the side of her face. I was pretty embarrassed to have been asked, but even more so because she wanted me to sign her face. "No," I told her, "I can't sign your face. Give me something else to sign."

She looked and looked and couldn't find anything. I suggested a program, piece of paper, maybe a t-shirt, anything. I was sweating from the game, but also because we were at an impasse. No way was I going to sign her face. Finally, we settled on her arm. I remember thinking how complicated signing autographs could be, but none have been that way since.

Michael Irvin
DALLAS COWBOYS

The 11th player chosen in the 1988 draft, Michael fought through tough injuries his first three seasons to become Troy Aikman's best weapon in the potent Dallas offense. Michael has led the Cowboys in both receptions and yardage the past three seasons and has become one of the best receivers in all of football. Appropriately called "The Playmaker," Michael has been to three Pro Bowls, and will undoubtedly appear in many more.

I am the quiet type who tries not to get approached too often, but I like the little kids. They have that look in their eye, like they're always up to something. There's something about the genuine smile of a small child when they look up at you. It's a very special feeling.

Athletes and Autographs

Hale Irwin
GOLF

With 20 PGA Tour victories, including three US Open titles, Hale is one of the greatest golfers of modern times. He has been a member of five Ryder Cup teams, including the most exciting contest in Ryder Cup history in 1992 when he outlasted Bernhard Langer. He has won a total of nine international events and was a standout defensive back in college at the University of Colorado.

As a golfer, you are accessible to the fans. In other sports, you walk off the court, or field and retire into a locker room. In golf, you retire directly into the public. There is no protected haven, and the public gets a chance to meet you and you them.

Nothing surprises me any more, but one time I was in Tokyo to play in the US-Japan matches. I went out shopping one day, and as I was walking down the streets of downtown Tokyo, I noticed this car that started honking.

I didn't think that it was directed at me, but the honking went on and on amidst all of the other noise that goes on in a big city like that. Finally, the car stopped right in the middle of traffic— which is no small feat— two people got out and approached me with a souvenir program from the tournament I was playing in. They saw me and wanted my autograph, right there on the streets of downtown Tokyo, which is as far away from a golf course as you can get.

Mark Jackson
INDIANA PACERS

The former 1987 Rookie of the Year as a New York Knick, Mark played for the Clippers before coming to the Pacers in the 1994 off-season. Mark, a tremendous passer and court general, looks forward to passing the ball to Reggie Miller when he is reunited in Indy with his former coach in Los Angeles, Larry Brown.

I never ever thought that anyone would want my autograph. Each time I receive a request, I am flattered. Growing up in New York around so many stars, I never thought that anyone would look at me like that. It's humbling because it shows me how far I have come in my own life. It's a tremendous compliment, and I thank God for it.

I collect some autographs— only of incredible people, like Muhammad Ali. He is a man that has done as much for mankind as he has for boxing. I have a jacket that he signed that was a part of a special collection. But I don't have his personal autograph where I met him and asked for it. If I did meet him, I would be taken away, because I've admired and respected him since I was a kid. His influence on me was indescribable. There is no question that his example will always live on.

Rickey Jackson
SAN FRANCISCO 49ERS

After 13 seasons with the Saints, where he established team records for sacks (123), games played (195) and fumble recoveries (26), Rickey joined the 49ers in a bid to go to the Super Bowl. Along with Richard Dent, Jackson chases the only active player with more career sacks, Reggie White. A quick, strong pass rusher, Rickey also excels at stopping the run. He is a Pro Bowl performer, and widely recognized as one of the best linebackers of his era.

Autographs for me are a home and away deal— just like football. When I'm back in my hometown in Florida, people never ask me for my autograph. Michael Jackson, even Michael Jordan himself, could walk down the middle of the street and no one would ever think of asking for an autograph. No would ever bother anyone in that small town. On the other hand, when I'm with the team, people always ask for autographs. That's understandable, fans are loyal and it's a way to show their enthusiasm.

Sign Language

Tom Jackson
ESPN

An original member of Denver's famous "Orange Crush" defense, Tom was an outstanding linebacker for the Broncos. Tom is an expert analyst for ESPN football segments and co-host of their NFL Prime Time show with Chris Berman, Robin Roberts and Joe Theisman.

I was a college Freshman at Louisville and had never signed an autograph before in my life. I had scored a touchdown in this one game and the next week went to a basketball game, the big sport at Louisville. As I was walking out, someone said, "Mr. Jackson, Mr. Jackson, can I have your autograph?" I looked around, because I thought that my father had shown up. To me, that was the only "Mr. Jackson" that I knew of. But Dad wasn't there. They were talking to me. I had never signed an autograph before or been referred to as "mister," so I signed the autograph and achieved two milestones in one brief moment.

Peter Jacobsen
GOLF

One of the most popular players on tour with fans, players and sponsors, this Pacific Northwest native is also one of golf's steadiest performers. Peter has won more than $3,000,000 and four PGA tournaments. He has also been a member of the prestigious Ryder Cup team and the winner of several foreign and non-tour events like the Enterprise Rent-A-Car challenge. An avid fan of the Portland Trailblazers, Peter once wore a Clyde Drexler jersey during a US Open round. A member of Jake Trout and the Flounders, Peter helped pen one of their better songs, "I Want a New Glove."

One time I found that signing autographs can be more hazardous than any sand trap. I was walking from a green to the next tee with my head down, signing autographs while focusing on the next hole. People were handing me the usual stuff: hats, visors, programs and I wasn't paying attention to the things that I was signing, because I was really focusing on what I needed to do on the next hole— that visualization thing that golfers talk about. All of a sudden— whammo— I ran into a tree branch, and it poked me in the eye. It was a direct hit, and it actually affected my vision for about a week thereafter. That's one of those things that can happen. I was simply going with the flow of people, just like I had done a thousand times before, concentrating on my next tee shot, and I got popped by the tree branch. I'd hate to go on the disabled list for signing an autograph, but it almost happened.

Sign Language

Haywood Jeffires
HOUSTON OILERS

The featured receiver in Houston's "run and shoot" offense, Haywood is only the second player to lead the AFC in receptions for three straight seasons. Haywood, a graduate of North Carolina State, is a Pro Bowl player and one of the few receivers ever to have caught more than 100 passes in a season.

This cute little girl, no older than three or four, came up to me one time, and told me that I was the greatest football player that she had ever seen. I responded by telling her that she was too young to even know what football was. She had a pen and piece of paper with her and she asked for my autograph. As I was signing she told me, "By the way, my daddy told me to tell you that, but please don't let him know that I told on him." I knew that some-body had put her up to it, because she was too young to know anything about the game of football. But I was impressed that this little girl could put all of those different thoughts together — especially that she knew that her father wouldn't want me to know that he masterminded her request. Kids really do learn at an early age.

Magic Johnson
LOS ANGELES LAKERS

When he has a basketball in his hands, there is no doubt that Earvin "Magic" Johnson is both magical and masterful. Magic brought a new dimension of skill and showmanship to competitive basketball that forever changed the landscape of the game. His five championship rings, three MVP awards, multiple All-Star and All-Pro honors understate his greatness. The second all-time NBA assist leader, Magic was All-NBA nine times and the playoff MVP recipient three times. His game, however, cannot be accurately described by statistics alone. Magic's incomparable ability to see the floor and elevate the play of his teammates and opponents is a tribute to his charisma and talents. Magic's career was fittingly capped with a Gold Medal performance as the captain of America's first "Dream Team" in the 1992 Olympics. Beloved worldwide, Magic is a part owner of the Lakers, worldwide basketball promoter, and a tireless worker for his charity, the Magic Johnson Foundation.

I've had so many things happen. Fans will do almost anything to get an autograph. Even when they see you in your car, they'll chase you on foot. It's like they believe they can catch you. Some people will run two, three blocks, full-speed just to ask for an autograph. When someone exerts that kind of effort— to show that they want it that bad, you usually end up signing for these people, also mainly to keep them from getting hit by a car.

Athletes and Autographs

Brent Jones
SAN FRANCISCO 49ERS

One of the keys to the 49ers' high octane offense, Brent's combination of speed, strength, smarts and sure hands has made him a Pro Bowl performer. Brent caught one of Joe Montana's last touchdown pass as a 49er and is a favorite target of Steve Young. A celebrity analyst of an excellent postgame television show on KGO, Brent's insight enlightens and entertains thousands of fans.

This guy saw me and started saying; "Hey, sign your card. Sign your card. Sign your card," as he waved this football card around. When I walked over to him, he handed me the card and I saw that it was Jerry Rice's football card. I told him, "I'm not Jerry Rice." "That's OK," he said, "I don't even know who he is." So at that point I decided that instead of signing my name, I would sign it, "Joe Montana," and that's what I did. I figured that anyone who doesn't know who Jerry Rice is wouldn't have a clue that I wasn't Joe Montana.

Athletes and Autographs

Henry Jones
BUFFALO BILLS

A strong force in the Bills' secondary, Henry is one of the AFC's big play performers. He led the conference in interceptions in 1992 and even returned two interceptions for touchdowns in one game against the Colts. Henry made the Pro Bowl after his second season, and looks forward to a long and productive career with the 4-time AFC champs.

At Super Bowl XXVII, this little girl walked up to me and told me that her grandfather used to sing a song to her about, "A Man Named Henry Jones." She must have been from Buffalo, because she said that when the Bills drafted me in 1991, it meant a great deal to her. It turns out that her grandfather died that year, and every time she sees the Bills play, she thinks of her grandfather and how he used to sing to her. As I was signing my name, she started to cry and told me how important her grandpa was to her, and that I reminded her of him. I don't know who sings that song, or even what the exact title is, but I'm looking forward to finding it someday. Maybe I can find the girl and send her a copy..."

My Moment With Michael

Not all interviews are conducted equally, and no interview was more difficult or rewarding than the one with Michael Jordan. I needed about 60 seconds with him, and he gave me at least 70.

When I arrived in Chicago, my friend Paul Hays told me; "If you don't get Michael Jordan's story - you don't have a book." Talk about pressure. And although I had already interviewed 100 athletes, I knew that Paul was right. Michael was "the man."

I arrived at Chicago Stadium four hours before tip-off. Nerves, poor knowledge of the city streets, and curiosity of the "Bulls Experience" had motivated me to get to Chicago Stadium early. I felt that things began well when some kids (youthful entrepreneurs, really) offered me "protection fees" to watch my Geo Metro for that evening's game against the Heat. Any time a car with more wheels than horsepower gets a little respect is always a harbinger of good fortune. And good fortune was the theme I wanted as I walked into the venerable home of "Da Bulls."

Looking for the court, I got pointed down a long hallway that I discovered ended with the Bulls' locker room. A guard outside informed me that it was too early to enter, and that no one was in there anyway. His directions to the court pointed me back down the hallway towards this gap that I had just passed. Once there, I was instructed to make an immediate right and proceed up the steps—then I would reach the arena floor.

I approached the gap, lowered my head to turn around the hairpin corner, and felt the subtle presence of an oncoming person. I turned the corner so abruptly that I had walked right into the oncoming person, except that he spun quickly out of the way the moment I was about to bump into his chest. Quickly looking up, I saw that it was Michael in a Malcolm X tank top. Smiling, he said, "That was close."

Here he was. I practically stepped on him, I had to talk to him, say something. So clutching my tape recorder, autograph sketch pad, notes, press pass and Geo Metro keys, I started to speak, "How's the swing, Michael?"

"Good," he responded. "Real good. Thanks for asking," His million dollar smile froze me in my tracks as he walked down towards the locker room.

I felt like Charlie Brown, having blown my chance to interview Jordan. The last person I had ever expected to see while lost in Chicago Stadium was Michael Jordan, and after running into him, all that I could think of saying was, "How's the swing?" What a choke job. My only consolation came in thinking that there would be several more chances to talk with him.

Wrong again.

Within ten seconds, a herd of reporters came pounding down the steps separating the court from the hallway, and they were all shouting for Michael. I soon realized that I was competing with something significantly larger than I had anticipated.

Another security guard came by and I asked him about Jordan's pregame routine and an appropriate time to approach him. "Man, he's gonna come up to shoot. But not to talk. For that, you gotta wait in a long line."

"So," I interjected, "interviewing him is going to be hard?" At this point I was more pleading for encouragement than asking for an assessment. "Well," he said, shaking his head, "Good luck."

Michael emerged thirty minutes later, a couple of security guards in tow, and headed for the court. Why the security guards, I wondered? Well, that question resolved itself as dozens of people saw him and descended upon his group, screaming at him, trying to divert his attention. The people yelling for him weren't fans— the game was hours away. They were stadium related people: concessionaires, security guards, maintenance workers and the like. I couldn't believe the volume of noise directed at him. I made a note of the reality of his celebrity, and the obvious prison of his popularity. He politely told people that he had to shoot, and that he'd be right back, but stopped to sign some things for a few people, take a picture and joke around with some familiar faces.

The fan in me told me that the court was the place to go. I would never be able to observe Einstein execute mathematical equations, or Lincoln draft a speech, but watching a solo performance by Michael was something that I should not pass up.

He shot in the dark of the empty facility, and effortlessly drained a mixture of shots. Free throws, spin moves, cross-over dribbles and three-pointers came in bunches, seamlessly choreographed by the greatest player in the game. I looked around, and noticed that no one else was enjoying the solo performance by this basketball virtuoso.

I was living millions of fans' sports fantasy, and felt that, at the very least, it would be a memorable legacy to my efforts to interview him.

The game itself was outstanding, with Jordan dominating the action early. From my press seat, I saw Jordan's trademark skills elevate the entire team. His talents even rubbed off on one young fan, Don Calhoun, who was chosen to participate in Coca-Cola's million dollar shot promotion during a game time-out.

Calhoun stepped up and threw in a 3/4 court shot to win himself $1,000,000 and the delirious applause of the fans and players. I was hoping that Mr. Calhoun's good fortune was yet another good sign for my interview aspirations.

As I approached the locker room for the post-game interviews, I felt upbeat and confident that somehow I would get my interview. But when I walked in and saw the installation of equipment before Jordan's locker area, I knew that I did not have any hope of talking to Jordan.

I felt that I should stay and watch, but I knew my only chance was to return to the hallway outside and hopefully talk to him as he left the locker room. I waited and waited. Richard Dent, the great defensive end was there. He, too, was waiting for Jordan. So we both waited. Finally, he came out, nattily attired and the screaming started: "Michaelllllllll !!! Michael!!!!!!" and that was by the reporters. He weaved his way through the throng of well-wishers, reporters, security and other onlookers.

I never had a chance in the hallway, so I went to the steps leading up to the court. All of the other players went this route, and I had hoped that Michael would follow suit. Sure enough, he did, and I wedged my way right into his path.

"Hey Michael, can I ask you a quick question?," I blurted. His eyes looked down, and he gave me that gentle nod, meaning "Go ahead, but please move you're practically standing on my feet."

So I went into my questioning routine, and somehow my screaming got his ear about the wavelength that everyone was using to attract his attention, and he said, "Uhh, my family is waiting for me— including my kids— so I can't answer that right now, but come back next game and I'll take care of you." And he was gone .

Still, I managed to talk to him. And that either said something for my luck, and/or persistence. Most importantly, he was truly courteous, especially considering the circumstances. Now, at least I had an idea what I was up against. I had one more chance to interview Michael. The Bucks game was two days away, giving me 48 hours to devise a plan.

The two days passed quickly— and this was my last chance. I concluded that my best opportunity was during his pregame routine. If I could somehow get lucky and stumble across his path while he was between his activities, I might just get my chance. I knew, however, that I as an individual, was overmatched. I might need some assistance to help me in my endeavor.

A friend of mine, Joe Hoffman, was working at the stadium, and he accompanied me. He and I waited outside the locker room entry where the players came in. "You'll know when he's here," I said, "because the screaming will start."

"Screaming?" Joe asked.

"Well, it's more or less a combination of both yelling and sceaming, but as soon as he comes out," I coached, "others are going to swarm him, so block them out and give me a clear path."

"Just how many people are you talking about?" Joe wanted to know.

"Well, it could be only one or two, but probably more," I estimated, watching the crowd of people build outside the locker room.

"I'm gonna need some help," Joe warned. "I don't think I can take more than one or two."

This whole thing was beginning to sound like an old western, but I had targeted some other people for last minute services. I had met some girls who sold concessions for the season ticket holders and I asked if they could run a little interference for us— only if we needed it. They were really nice and sympathetic to our cause, and said they would help.

Just then, the screaming started. I knew that Michael had parked his car and was moments away from the locker area.

"He's here!!," I blurted. "When the security guards open the door," I said, "cut in front of them so that I can talk to Michael."

Joe gave me that sarcastic look. "That should be real easy," he said. "All I have to do is cut in front of a highly skilled, paid security guard who is trying to protect the greatest athlete in the world. And I'm sure Michael will appreciate it."

I couldn't get Joe kicked out of the Stadium, I still needed his help. "You're right. We need to act in a civilized fashion." As soon as I finished my sentence, the door swung open, and Michael proceeded directly into the locker room.

"Hey Michael," I groveled, "can I please ask you a quick question?"

"Not right now, I have to get changed." With that, he disappeared into the protected haven of the Bulls' locker room.

Waiting for him to return, I remembered that my high school football coach once said, "Men, every play is a touchdown on the chalkboard. But once you get on the field, you'll find that it's easier to be an artist than a football player."

I hoped that wasn't the case with our loosely diagrammed, hastily prepared effort.

When the door opened, and Michael walked out, he was alone, but not unnoticed. A reporter briskly walked towards him, but Joe diverted his path long enough for me to initiate conversation first.

"Michael," I started, pulse quickening, "could I ask you a quick question?"

"OK— real quick," and he gestured to walk with him as he went to the court.

I knew that I had to move fast, because the floor was probably 30 seconds away, and Joe and my concessionaire friends were doing overtime getting in others' ways. I quickly asked; "Have you ever had any autograph requests or moments with fans that stick out in your mind?"

"Ahhh," I translated that as Air-Speak for "I'm thinking."

Michael's eyes focused, and he said, "Yeah" and recounted his story. He finished talking to me while tying his shoes, shook my hand and was gone...

My lasting impression of the whole process was of Jordan's incredible popularity and his handling of it. The demands on his time a vertical line, and the supply almost nonexistent, Michael somehow made it work. The pandemonium and screaming, requests for smiles, autographs and/or pictures were constants in Jordan's life.

Yet he managed to make the most of it. The three days that I observed him, Michael made a point to walk up to children, disabled people and shy, retiring types. Rather than bow his head down, a celebrity standard, Jordan's head was like a periscope zeroing in on the appropriate targets. Some burn victims were off to the left, he directs the mob that way. Fans in wheelchairs were on the right, he points the crowd their way. In my opinion, America's most celebrated figure was not only deserving of the attention, but up to the enormous, impossible expectations of the circumstances. There is no blueprint for Michael to follow, he seems to make it up as he goes along, and his genuine character makes every decision seem like the right one—just ask his fans.

We Americans tend to deify our celebrities, but after watching Michael Jordan for three days, I think that there is nothing wrong with those who do, indeed, want to "Be Like Mike." Both on and off the court, it's an impressive show to watch.

One More Thing...

As a final note to these thoughts about Michael Jordan and his celebrity, I have a friend, Chris, who came back from volunteering in Mongolia (population 2.2 million) and told me of the rural, remote life for the Mongolian herdsmen. The country citizens commute via horseback and when they come across fellow travellers, they dismount and share information about their respective journeys.

One day Chris was travelling in the countryside when his group encountered some native herdsmen going in the opposite direction. The travellers all dismounted and squatted in the regional fashion, shared some snuff and light conversation.

The talk finally turned to Chris. It was obvious that he was a foreigner. The strangers asked him where he came from.

"America," Chris offered in his best Mongolian accent.

"Ahh, America," remarked one of the robed, weathered herdsman, "Michael Jordan!"

Chris could only laugh. Even in one of the world's most remote and underdeveloped places, Michael Jordan is still a popular ambassador. Chris only wishes that Michael could have seen the cultural exchange. He thinks that Jordan would have gotten a big laugh as well. Furthermore, Mongolians don't ask for autographs. Maybe Michael might want to travel there. Apparently, a significant portion of the country looks like one big fairway.....

Sign Language

Michael Jordan
TWO SPORT STAR: BULLS & BARONS

The most popular athlete in the history of sports, Michael Jordan's accomplishments have transcended those of virtually every competitor from any era. A three-time league MVP, Michael led the NBA in scoring for seven consecutive seasons before he retired from basketball. More significantly, he spearheaded the Bulls' efforts in winning their three consecutive NBA titles. He scored more than 20,000 points in his career and is the only player ever to average more than 40 points per game in the NBA Finals. Voted both the NBA's most valuable Offensive and Defensive Player on numerous occasions, Jordan undoubtedly would have been the league's "Transitional Player of the Year" if they had such an honor. Michael also has two Gold Medals as a Olympian, an NCAA Championship game-winning shot as a collegian at North Carolina, and a significant role in the attendance records of his minor league team, the Birmingham Barons. No level of eloquence could accurately describe his style of play, but every future athlete will forever strive to reach the new standards of competitive performance that he set.

I was playing in a summer league, and this lady saw me come out of the gym and watched me get in my car. So she jumped in front of my car and laid down and wouldn't get up until I gave her an autograph. I couldn't believe that she wanted it that bad, but she did— and I gave it to her. I get a lot of requests and in a lot of places, but the kids are the best ones to sign for. Sometimes they get crowded out by adults, and I wish that wasn't the case, because they're the ones who will keep the memory for a long time.

Jim Kelly
BUFFALO BILLS

One of the best passers in the league, Jim is a sure Hall-of-Famer after his tremendous career with the Bills concludes. A strong-armed, gutsy quarterback, Jim also has the touch required to be an elite passer. Originally a USFL Houston Gambler, Jim has thrown for over 26,000 yards and 175 touchdowns as a Bill while amassing a 86% quarterback rating. Jim's quarterback roots are deep. He comes from the fertile western Pennsylvania area which produced other passers like Marino, Montana, Namath and Unitas. He attended the University of Miami, and started the great passing tradition at that college football powerhouse. The Bills' leader in virtually every meaningful quarterback statistic, Jim is still hungry to bring the Super Bowl trophy back to Buffalo. He is determined to do just that and continues to fight through injuries in order to accomplish that objective.

When I was a kid, I was in a punt, pass and kick competition, and I met Terry Bradshaw. I made sure to take a picture with him, because he was one of my heroes at the time. I still have the picture, and years later when I got to know him, I brought the old one that we had taken years before, and asked him to sign it. He wrote under it, "This picture was taken ten years ago, and as you can see, when both quarterbacks had a lot more hair." That goes to show that all quarterbacks find a way to laugh.

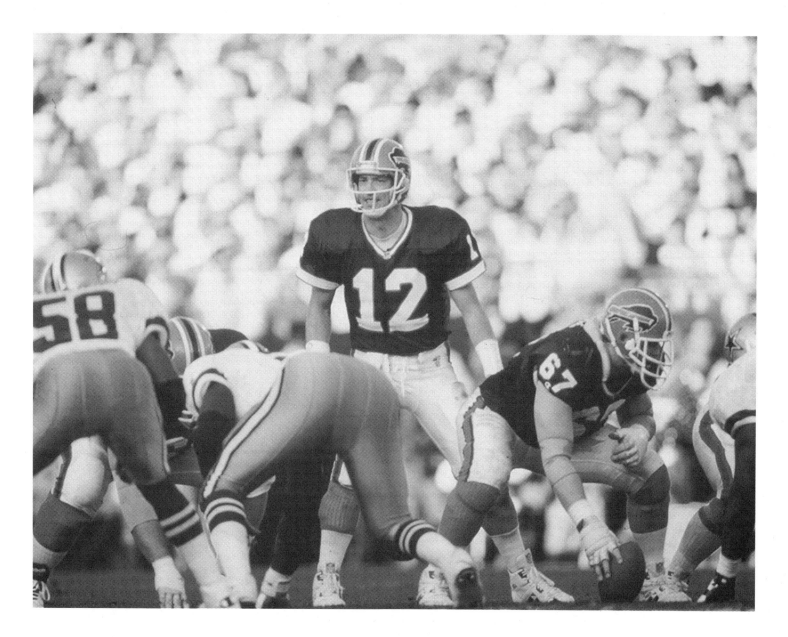

Athletes and Autographs

Shawn Kemp
SEATTLE SUPERSONICS

The most explosive player in the NBA, Shawn brings charisma, energy and spectacular creativity to his game. Shawn is the focal point of the Sonics' powerful offense and stingy defense. A former first round pick of the Sonics, Shawn's style of play has made him one of America's most popular athletes. A two time All-Star, Shawn was a core member of Don Nelson's "Dream Team II."

People always recognize you— in elevators, in your car, at restaurants— everywhere. It's hard for people to imagine what it feels like to have a large group of people gather around you. It's something that you get used to and a situation where it helps to be tall. I didn't expect to be an NBA player, so just being here is a surprise. And I've learned that if you make a name for yourself, people want to meet you. Getting an autograph is the way they prove that they've met you.

In LA, some celebrities want to meet you, and that seems funny, because growing up I always wondered what it would be like to meet them. I get a lot of mail. Sometimes up to 500 letters a day. My mom helps me take care of that. It's an important job, and I wouldn't trust anyone else to help me go through it and respond to the fans.

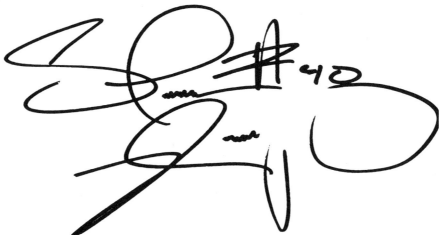

Sign Language

Cortez Kennedy
SEATTLE SEAHAWKS

The third player selected in the 1990 draft, Cortez has established himself as the most dominant nosetackle in the NFL. Cortez, a former All-American from the University of Miami, was honored as the league's Defensive Player of the Year. He is the anchor for the entire Seahawk defense.

The most memorable autograph I signed was the very first one. After my first game at Miami, this little boy came up to me and asked me to sign for him. I was so excited, I did it in a hurry. It took me forever to come down to earth— I was that excited. That first one was a great feeling. I had come from a junior college in a really small town. I never thought that anyone would ask me for my autograph. I thought that it only happened to movie stars. I don't get excited like that anymore, but I'm still signing as long as they're asking.

Jason Kidd
DALLAS MAVERICKS

A two time All-American at the University of California of Berkeley, Jason Kidd was selected with the second overall pick of the 1994 draft. A playing legend since grammar school, Jason is a rare athlete whose skills are defined by teamwork, defense and creative artistry. Jason's instinctive ability to find the open man and apply full court defensive pressure are only two of the qualities that make him a star. The future cornerstone to the Mavericks' franchise, this humble hero avoids comparisons the other great players and lets his play on the court define his game.

I love to sign autographs, because I know that fans make my career possible. They're my support group, and I try to reverse the role when someone approaches me for an autograph, 'cause I know what it's like to look up to people and want to meet them. Truthfully, it's humbling to think that people would care that much to even ask. Celebrity and autographs are a great part of being an athlete. Because I can play ball, I've met people like Joe Montana and Magic Johnson. I grew up watching Joe play football, winning Super Bowls, MVP awards, playing hurt, coming back from injuries and showing the courage it takes to be a champion. Magic is my idol—and to say that I know him is like a dream come true. So when someone seems happy to meet me, I certainly know the feeling.

Stacey King
MINNESOTA TIMBERWOLVES

A former first round pick of the Bulls, Stacey came to the T'Wolves in a trade for Luc Longley. He is the prototypical low post scoring specialist. A former All-American from Oklahoma, Stacey is looking to become a leader of the improving T'Wolves.

I was a rookie when I met Dr. J. I immediately asked him for his autograph. I grew up being a big fan of his, and I never thought that I would get close to him, much less ever meet him. I wish that I could've played with him, but simply meeting him and getting his autograph was such a big deal. I was so excited— I couldn't even speak. That feeling is something that I see in the kids' faces when I meet them. I had that exact feeling ..... Dr. J— Wow!!!

I love little kids. It takes a lot of courage to approach an athlete and ask for an autograph. By meeting them, you can affect their lives because they are going to tell all of their friends and family that they met you. Knowing that, I always try to be positive, and it gives me as good a feeling as it gives them. If I can make a little kid feel like Dr. J made me feel as an adult—that's great.

Sign Language

Tom Kite
GOLF

One of the greatest golfers of all time, Tom has won 19 PGA tournaments, including the 1992 US Open at Pebble Beach. Tom, who has won the Ryder Cup an astounding seven times, has also won more money ($8,000,000) than any other player in the history of the game. Tom has also won two Vardon trophies, two Arnold Palmer trophies and a Bob Jones award. A true student of the game as well as a great champion, Texan Tom is a disciple of famed author Harvey Penick.

I was doing an outing in Seoul, Korea with John Daly, and we walked out of the clubhouse with the gentleman we were with. One of the men had a Testerosa parked out front, and we were looking at it, admiring it. He then asked John and I to sign it for him. So I signed the driver's seat, and John the passenger seat. Given our games, it should have been the other way around. But somewhere in Korea, there's a beautiful Testerosa going around with autographs on its nice leather seats.

Tony Kubek
NEW YORK YANKEES

One of the best shortstops in franchise history, Tony left the field in the 60s and went straight to the broadcast booth. Truly a winner, Tony retired having won five World Series rings in nine productive seasons with the Yankees. An insightful analyst with a great appreciation and understanding of the game, Tony explains baseball as well as anyone.

In my day there weren't any shows, dealers, card shops and things of that sort. People didn't put a price on autographs, so there wasn't the demand for the stuff that you see today. If a fan had a signature on something, it meant that he got it by running into the player himself at the ballpark.

I had the opportunity to watch Roger Maris and Mickey Mantle go after Babe Ruth's record in 1961, and those guys couldn't do anything without being swamped by people. They couldn't go out to eat, or out on the town. They had to stay in their rooms. It was the only way to avoid the huge crowds of people that instantly surrounded them. I don't know what it's like for Michael Jordan, but I doubt that he goes through what those guys went through in chasing Babe Ruth's single season home run record. In New York, with all of the media coverage and hype around that Yankee team, those guys were mobbed everywhere they went. The press scrutinized and chronicled their every move. The pressure was unbelievable. I don't know if there has ever been anything like that where two guys on the same team were gunning for the same historic record.

Christian Laettner
MINNESOTA TIMBERWOLVES

What was Christian Laettner's greatest accomplishment of 1992? Being named college player of the year? Scoring the most dramatic shot in the history of college basketball, a last second jumpshot to beat Kentucky in the NCAA Semifinals? Playing on the first Dream Team in Barcelona and winning the gold medal in basketball? Appearing on David Letterman's show and demonstrating the ability to walk on his hands? Obviously, it had to be meeting Dave, Paul and the rest of the show crew. Either that or establishing himself as a premier power forward in the NBA as a consistent double figure scorer and effective rebounder.

Nothing specific stands out because there are so many requests (for my autograph). It would be like trying to remember every day of my life. It's simply another part of the day-to-day life of a basketball player— and some days are different than others. Some days I get 500 requests and other days I'll get two.

A lot of people would think that Barcelona was an intense scene, but it wasn't. The biggest frenzy was at Duke after the last National Championship. Duke fans are the most intense basketball fans that I have seen, and going through that prepared me for the spotlight of being an NBA player.

Bob Lanier
NBA HALL OF FAME

One of the best centers of his era, Bob collected more than 20,000 points as a Detroit Piston and Milwaukee Buck. Bob, who has been heavily involved with the NBA's "Stay in School" program since his retirement, spent several years giving motivational speeches to youngsters across the country. Currently an assistant coach with the Golden State Warriors, Bob is still notorious for having the biggest shoe in the NBA (size 22).

There is not one specific memory associated with an autograph. If anything, it confuses me why one individual would want another individual's signature. Autographs for athletes are a way of life. Sometimes obliging an autograph request is a necessary evil. As somebody who signs, I always wonder where the autograph goes. It seems to me that once the fan gets it, it just ends up in a drawer somewhere.

We have a problem today with distortion. We athletes are just human beings like everyone else. Our value get distorted by the fans. Just because we are doing something they admire does not mean that having our autograph is a great accomplishment. The important thing about anyone is character, self esteem, how people earn respect. Those are important things to acquire— not an autograph.

If you admire someone and want to meet them, sticking something in their face and asking them to sign it is not the right way to meet someone. There is no real exchange there. If kids want to idolize celebrities, they need to look at the person and find out if they are truly people who should be idolized. Do these athletes or celebrities have the necessary character and integrity to make all facets of their lives work? Kids shouldn't admire athletes for their physical skills— those eventually go away. They should admire those who have mental skills, because they last forever.

Steve Larmer
NEW YORK RANGERS

One of the NHL's most durable players, Steve is also one of its best defensemen. A longtime Blackhawk, Steve's presence in the Ranger lineup solidified it with veteran leadership and helped lead them to their first Stanley Cup in more than 50 years.

The only place that I ever get asked to sign is around the rink. And I don't mind signing for our fans— they're real good to us. I don't think that I could live like a Wayne Gretzky. If I were forced to live with the threat of being recognized everywhere I went, I might choose to live in a closet. For me, hockey's hockey and the rest of my life is my own. I'm just a regular Joe just like everybody else. I'm thankful, honestly, for my anonymity, and I value the fact that I blend in.

Frank Layden
UTAH JAZZ

The former coach of the Jazz and current General Manager of the franchise, Frank is one of the keenest minds in the NBA. He masterminded the drafting of Karl Malone and John Stockton, two Dream Team stars. Frank is also one of the funniest personalities in the NBA.

I was in London, England, and this American walks up to me and asks for an autograph. "Sure," I said, "I'll sign," and then I signed my name.

The guy looks at the autograph, then looks up at me and asks; "What did you sign there?"

"Frank Layden," I said.

"Frank Layden?," he said. "I thought that you were Tip O'Neill."

Sign Language

Luc Longley
CHICAGO BULLS

Originally drafted by the Timberwolves, Luc was traded to Chicago for Stacey King in the '93-94 season. A native of Australia, Luc starred at New Mexico before becoming a solid NBA big man.

There are always people with obscure angles...sending their children up to you to get autographs for them and even writing letters asking for a ball, jersey and two pictures that are personalized. "And by the way, could you send it Express Mail?" Some requests do ask for a lot, and they don't even bother to send a return envelope. So I write and tell them to go out, buy the stuff and ship it to me in a box. Otherwise, I can't chase all of the things down for them.

In Australia, you don't sign as much. Probably because only 16 million people live there— as opposed to the 250 million here in the states. My first autograph was at a high school tournament in Tasmania. I was only 15, but an adult asked me. As a kid, I felt that I had to sign for him.

Davis Love III
GOLF

One of the longest hitters on tour, Davis is also one of its best players. He has won seven tournaments, and almost $4,000,000 in his young career. An aggressive competitor with the skill to match, Davis has been a Ryder Cup, Dunhill Cup, Walker Cup and World Cup team member.

I was playing in the Bay Hill tournament in Orlando, and I had an afternoon tee time one day. This gave me time to go out for brunch with my family before my round. We were at a Friday's restaurant, and this lady approached me under the impression that I'm John Cook, another tour player.

"Mr. Cook," she asked, "Can I please have your autograph?"

"Well," I told her, "I'm not John Cook, but I'll give you my autograph."

At that point she insisted; "Yes, you are John Cook!"

"Look ma'am," I said, repeating myself, " I'm not John Cook. My name is Davis Love. I also play golf."

Then she got stubborn, "You are too John Cook, because I've seen you on TV."

Now I'm getting just as stubborn as she, "John has an injured wrist and is in California at the moment in a cast. So, not only is he not playing in the tournament in town, he's not playing anywhere at the moment, and I am Davis Love."

She then got mad, returned to her table and informed all of her friends that I'm John Cook and very rude. She then proceeded to glare at me for the rest of the meal and give me the evil eye. To this day, John has an enemy in Orlando that he does not deserve.

The only time when I won't sign is during a round. Some fans don't understand that, but it would be like a baseball player signing between innings. And if you sign for one person and not the others because you need to go and tee off, then you feel like you let somebody down. For the fans, deep down, it's not the actual autograph that is important, it's still about getting close to the athlete. I understand that.

Danny Manning
PHOENIX SUNS

The first pick in the 1988 draft, Danny has become an All-Star and scoring leader in his brief NBA career, averaging almost 19 points per game. Danny is one of the principal threats in the Suns' balanced attack. Having led the Jayhawks of Kansas to the National Championship in his collegiate years, Danny hopes to be the key ingredient to the Suns' future title aspirations in the pros. His father, Ed, was a professional basketball player and Danny's role model growing up.

When you're 6'10", people tend to know that you're somebody, so they'll ask you to sign even if they are not sure exactly who you are. After we won the National Championship over Oklahoma, some people slipped me some pieces of paper to sign in class. Hey, in the classroom, I was just a student trying to learn the material like everyone else and I was signing autographs! As a kid, I collected lots of Julius Ervings' autographs because my dad played with him. I had a few and stockpiled them. But now I don't collect anything. I give all of my memorabilia away.

Dan Marino
MIAMI DOLPHINS

A first round draft pick from Pitt, Dan stepped out of the collegiate ranks and right into the NFL record books. He is one of only three quarterbacks ever to pass for more than 40,000 yards, and he is closing in on virtually every major passing record. He has completed more than 300 touchdown passes and is the owner of a slew of records. He has thrown for over 3,000 yards for nine consecutive seasons, and topped the 4,000 yardage mark five times. In 1984, he set the single season marks for yardage (5,084) and touchdows (48). Dan has thrown for four or more touchdown passes in a game 17 times and has the most games (10) of 400 passing yards on his way to seven Pro Bowls. Sidelined by a ruptured Achilles tendon in 1993, Dan worked hard to make it back for the '94 season.

I was eating dinner in a restaurant, and this guy approached me and asked me to sign something for him. I politely told him to wait for the end of the meal, and then I would be glad to sign. So fifteen minutes later, the same guy walks up to me and says, " OK, I'm finished with my meal now, could you sign this for me now?" Obviously, he thought that I'd be willing to give him an autograph when he was finished eating. I started to laugh and told him that he must have misunderstood me, because I meant that I would sign after I had finished my meal. He kind of looked at me cross-eyed, and I laughed at the humorous nature of the misunderstanding. So I signed what he wanted me to sign and had a good laugh the rest of the meal.

Athletes and Autographs

Don Mattingly
NEW YORK YANKEES

A six time All-Star and seven time Gold Glove winner, Don is one of the greatest players ever to wear the Yankee pinstripes. He holds the record for most grand slams in a season (six), and is tied with Steve Garvey and Wes Parker for baseball's top fielding percentage at first base (.995). The AL MVP in 1985, Don is one of baseballs most popular players. He is also the first Yankee captain since the late Thurman Munson.

At Spring training one year, there was this one guy who waited for me every day to sign things for him. Every day, he never missed a day, and he'd always have different things for me to sign. After about four or five days, he kind of irritated me, because he was following me down the street, chasing me in parking lots and things like that. But it turned out that he was a real nice guy, and over the course of spring training, I got to like him. It was almost like I was waiting to see him every day just to say "Hi." I practically knew him by name. It was a different type of experience, because I went through the whole spectrum of emotions with this guy, from not knowing him at all, to being a bit irritated, to actually liking him because he was pretty pleasant. Most autograph seekers you see only once, but this guy was a part of my daily ritual.

When I was a kid growing up in Evansville (Indiana), we didn't have a major league team, so I didn't really collect autographs. But they had a AAA team, and I used to work over there a little bit. We didn't collect the players' autographs, but we used to use their gloves, bats and balls and just have a great time. For a kid, that was the ultimate— getting to play with professional equipment on that beautiful field. Of course, we didn't get to keep the equipment, but just having the chance to use it was fun. Now, I collect some autographs for my kids. I get a few balls and things like that signed by some of the guys, and I store it in a closet for them. Maybe someday they'll be interested in the memorabilia of some of the people that I played with and against.

Guy McIntyre
GREEN BAY PACKERS

A five time Pro Bowler, Guy is one of the best linemen in the NFL. Fast, strong and durable, Guy's presence is anathema to any lurking defensive player. Guy made a reputation for his athletic style of play at the University of Georgia, where famed announcer Larry Munson would say, "Go, Hershel, Go!" as Guy toiled down field.

After playing in a softball game in Oakland, a guy walked up to me and said that he had something personal that he wanted signed. "So," I asked him, "What is it?" He then handed me a brassiere and a pen. I asked him if the bra belonged to him and he laughed and told me that it was his girlfriend's. So I signed it, and to this day that is the only Guy McIntyre officially autographed bra in the entire world.

Mark McGwire
OAKLAND ATHLETICS

A six time All-Star and former Olympian, Mark burst onto the professional scene in 1987 by establishing the MLB record for most home runs as a rookie (49). He was the unanimous selection for top rookie honors that year and has since followed that debut by becoming one of baseball's top players. Mark is the first player in Major League history to have hit 30 or more home runs his first four seasons, and he is the fifth fastest player to hit 200 career homers (Ruth, Kiner, Killebrew and Matthews were the first four) A tremendous fielder, Mark won a Gold Glove award in 1991.

I saw Jerry Seinfeld perform when I was in college, and I liked him right away. His brand of humor, delivery, all of that. A few years ago, before Jerry had his TV show, I was in Minnesota eating dinner, and in walks Seinfeld and a friend. He walks right up to me and said, "I just wanted to meet you and shake your hand." For the first time in my life, I was speechless. I couldn't even invite him to sit down and join us. I really was that speechless. I kept thinking to myself, "Geez, this is Jerry Seinfeld— right here." We chatted for a few minutes, and he went off and ate. I talked with the waiter and told him that I wanted Jerry's check. I was going to buy him and his buddy dinner. It was the least that I could do. So I did and left.

Anyway, a year and a half goes by, his show is a big hit, and I'm in LA with a friend eating lunch. Again, Jerry walks into the restaurant. This time, he's with his agent. He comes up to me, "Mark, how ya' doin'? Great to see you." And we talked for a while, before he goes and eats. I finished my meal, and wanted to leave. I asked the waiter for my bill. "Jerry picked it up," the waiter said. "He's getting you back." That's not a story about autographs, but about recognition, which is the basis for things like autographs. Here's a guy, a real Hollywood celebrity, who happens to like baseball. I'm a baseball player, who has always loved comedy, and we first recognized each other because of our respective professions.

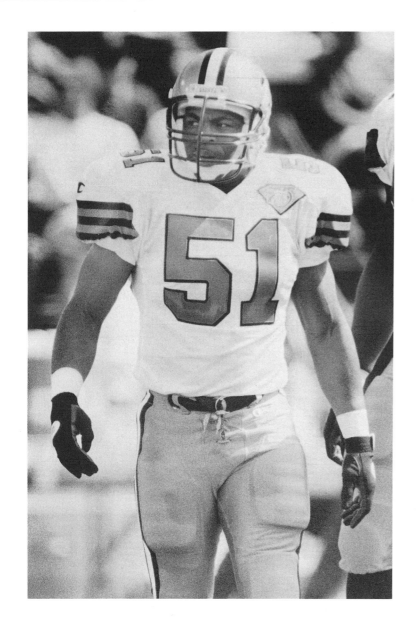

Sign Language

Sam Mills
NEW ORLEANS SAINTS

One of the last remaining defensive NFL players with USFL experience, Sam is still one of the NFL's premier inside linebackers. Sam, an intuitive player who gets by on both ability and smarts, has been the leader of the impressive Saints defense for many years. At 5'9", Sam is one of the smaller inside players, but he has shown that he does not lack in heart and has been rewarded with four Pro Bowl selections.

When people first started asking me for my autograph, I could only wonder why anyone would ever want it— it's only me, Sam Mills. I still sometimes feel that way, especially when people that I've known for years ask me to sign something for them. When I give an autograph to a friend, I feel awkward because a friend is acting like a fan. I know that my friends don't share that perspective, but I always feel uncomfortable signing for them. I guess it's because I don't want my friends to be like regular fans, I want them to be my friends first. I am the same Sam that I have been for years, and I don't want them to look at me like I'm just a professional athlete.

One situation that I like is when I hear from kids whose fathers I have played with at one time or another. I make sure to respond to those kids and sign something for them, because I don't want them to think that their dads are lying to them. No kid should think that their father is a liar. I always make sure to write that I enjoyed playing with their father and please send him my best wishes. Those autographs make me feel the best because I am identifying with a father and his child.

Chris Miller
LOS ANGELES RAMS

Along with Bill Musgrave, Chris rewrote the record books at the University of Oregon before becoming a star with the Atlanta Falcons. Injuries slowed him in Atlanta, where he had passed for over 85 touchdowns and 14,000 yards and earned a trip to the Pro Bowl. He went to the Rams in 1994 to become the cornerstone of their future. Chris, an avid golfer, frequently appears in charity and celebrity events. He has even played at Augusta National, a sports dream for any athlete.

I was with the Falcons, and we had just beaten New Orleans in a playoff game. This gal found me in the Atlanta airport, and she had an unusual request. I was trying to avoid the throng of people that were around, and I had found a back way to go through the terminal when she came up to me and asked me to sign both parts of her chest— if you can imagine that. I signed, but without peeking. She was really polite. And if she wasn't, there is no way that I could've signed. I signed as fast as I could so that she wouldn't see how nervous and awkward I felt.

Harold Miner
MIAMI HEAT

Nicknamed "Baby Jordan" because of his spectacular leaping ability, Harold has not disappointed those who anointed him with such high expectations. Harold won his first slam dunk competition in Utah and expects to entertain and wow more fans in his immediate future. He also became the first player since Lew Alcindor in Pac-10 history to score 2,000 points.

I was in college, taking a test, and these kids came to the classroom looking to get my autograph. They were about 10 or 11 years old and just showed up out of no-where. I told them that I couldn't sign until the test was over, so they went outside and waited for me to finish my exam. They waited for about an hour, and when I finished, they were still outside waiting for me. I gave them my autograph.

One thing that I didn't anticipate about the pros was that you need to be careful about what you sign. So many people put so many things in front of you, and half the time, you don't even know what you are signing. Coming into the league, the older guys helped by telling me what to look out for, but some people are crazy and they'll stick all sorts of things in front of you.

Joe Montana
KANSAS CITY CHIEFS

The greatest quarterback in the history of the game, Joe Montana's football exploits are heroic, inspiring and legendary. Much like other great athletes, the statistics of his career only tell a small part of his story.. A winner of winners, Joe has three Super Bowl MVP awards and is that game's all-time leading passer with a 127.8% rating. Beyond his objective numeric accomplishments, Joe is known for his abilities to read defenses as if they were billboards and to recover from serious injury. The courage, leadership and modesty of one the greatest athletes ever are characteristics that fans and fellow athletes admire and cheer.

When I was with the 49ers, kids used to follow me from where I came out of the players' parking lot, all the way along this fenced area and out into the flow of cars. After watching me being chased on the field all day, these kids adopted that defensive lineman mentality and ran after me. I'd see them trying really hard to catch up to ask me, and I'd feel bad that they were running so hard— so I'd pull over and try to give them an autograph. It got to be a part of the game routine every year.

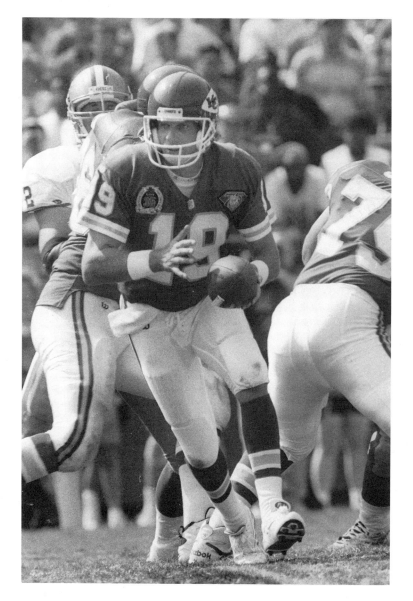

Athletes and Autographs

Warren Moon
MINNESOTA VIKINGS

Warren is not only one of the best quarterbacks in football, he is one of the league's most highly respected players. Originally a CFL superstar, Warren played for the Oilers for many years before going to the Vikings. As an Oiler, he established career marks for passing yards (33,685) and touchdowns (196). He also holds the NFL record for passes attempted (655) and completed (404) in a single season (1991). A graduate of the University of Washington, Warren is a perennial passing leader and Pro Bowl participant. Most importantly, Warren devotes a significant amount of time to charitable causes.

I've played a long time and over the years, signed thousands of things for thousands of people. I don't mind signing as long as I'm not eating or watching a basketball game, or any other sporting event. In both cases, I always ask the person to come back when I'm through eating, or when there is a time-out in the action. Once at the NFL Experience promotion, I was signing for a large group of people when a woman approached me and asked me to sign her baby's diaper. I didn't know how to approach that one, but I was willing to try. The mother said that it would be easy as she bent the child over to me and showed me his bottom. And I signed right there—right there on his little bottom!

#1

Wholly Moses!

In interviewing basketball teams, it always seemed that I was following the Milwaukee Bucks. No matter what town I was in, so were the Bucks. Our colliding itineraries made me feel like either a beat writer or some sort of journalistic groupie.

I was always a Buck fan. Having lived in Milwaukee as a boy, the first professional basketball game I attended featured two gentlemen named Oscar Robertson and Lew Alcindor, so the green and white were always a welcome sight. The 1993 Bucks, however, were not to be confused with the 1971 team.

The 1993 team had a good nucleus of young players, a great coach and a lot of promise. They also had a future Hall-of-Famer named Moses Malone on the roster. The great center's career started in the ABA and had taken him through Houston, Philadelphia, Atlanta and Washington. His biography in the media guide was a small book in itself. He had won three league MVP awards, multiple All-Pro designations and collected a batch of records and accolades. I always liked his tireless, persistent work ethic on the offensive boards, and I really wanted to interview him.

In approaching venerable stars, I always felt that their patience had been worn a bit thin over the years, so I always tried to be polite. After a few limited conversations with Moses, I didn't come away with a qualified interview, but I wouldn't be surprised if he moonlights for *Mad Magazine*, writing the "Snappy Answers to Stupid Questions" section.

The first conversation in Los Angeles went like this:

"Hey Moses," I started, "can I ask you a question?"

"Yeah, you just did," and he walked away.

Strike one. Give the Hall-of-Famer a "harrumph."

Afterwards, I interviewed Doc Rivers in Phoenix and he told me the story that appears in this book about Moses signing for the shivering fan who waited for the team plane to arrive during a New Jersey snow storm. But Moses made a point to emphasize that this was an exception, and it became a source for Rivers' amusement. When Doc related the story to me, I had an idea that Moses' last autograph may have been to that kid in New Jersey.

But it gave me an idea...

A few weeks later in Milwaukee, I approached Moses. Notebook in hand, I smiled at him and said, "Hey Moses, I heard a story about you."

He cocked his head, thought for a split second and looked at me, anticipating the effect of his response. "True," he said and walked away.

Strike two.

A couple of days later, I saw Moses in Chicago. This time, I was determined to get a little more conversational exchange from him. I knew that I wouldn't get an autograph story from him, but I wanted to see if I could momentarily engage him in real conversation.

"Say Moses," I began, "somone said that you were a scrofulous kind of guy..."

"Scrofu-what?", he said.

I knew I had him for at least a second. "Yeah," I added, "but I made him take it back."

Moses gave me a small smile and a sidelong glance. "Thanks, tough guy. You're still not getting an interview."

Strike three. This time, we both walked away.

Terry Mulholland
NEW YORK YANKEES

A hard-throwing left-hander, Terry is a mainstay of the Yankee rotation. Originally a member of the San Francisco Giants, Terry later pitched for the Phillies and distinguished himself by throwing a no-hitter and by starting the 1993 All-Star game. A consistent, high-effort player, Terry once struck out 14 players in one game, a career high.

I got a letter from a boy in Long Island who happened to be named Terry Mulholland also. He sent me some cards and asked if I would sign them. I never wondered if Mulholland was a popular name, but I signed the cards, sent him a note which wished him well and that was all.

Chris Mullin
GOLDEN STATE WARRIORS

A five time All-Star and two time Olympic gold medalist, Chris Mullin is one of the greatest basketball players of his generation. Chris was the Warriors' first round pick in the 1985 draft after winning the John Wooden award for being the best college player. Since then, he has been their unquestioned team leader, averaging over 22 points per game. Voted first team All-NBA in 1992, Chris was the Dream Team's second leading scorer at the Barcelona Olympics. A fabulous passer and team player, Chris is a true superstar.

Growing up, I never collected autographs or thought about being a celebrity. It was all about playing ball. I knew that if I got an autograph, it would be lost by the time I got home. I look at the autograph request as a privilege— a validation. But like anything else, there's a time and place for it, so sometimes I can't accommodate a request. If coach wants me on the floor in five minutes, I can't tell him that I need to sign autographs. I'm supposed to be on the court. All athletes have to stick to their schedules, so you sometimes feel guilty if you can't sign and don't have the time to explain it to a fan.

It's a whole different business now, because it literally is a business. When I came into the league, cards weren't a big deal. Now, they're huge. The differences between the Olympics in '84 and Barcelona were incredible. I couldn't believe the growth of basketball's popularity in those eight years. The added attention isn't necessarily a bad thing, as long as it's in moderation. Too much of a good thing isn't always a good thing. You can be the twelfth man on the worst team, and people will still recognize you because each game is on TV. Everyone has a card, and the fans are up on the latest news. Now, sometimes sports is the main news. But sports shouldn't change the way you are. You've got to be yourself. If you're in a popular profession and what you do brings some good into another's life— that's great— but it doesn't mean that it should change you. You have to respect both others and yourself.

Sign Language

Larry Nance
CLEVELAND CAVALIERS

An All-American at Clemson, Larry burst onto the NBA scene as an All-Star for the Phoenix Suns where he became the winner of the very first Slam Dunk contest. He has scored over 15,000 points, hauled down 7,000 rebounds and swatted more than 1,000 shots so far in his career. An intimidating shot blocker, Larry retired after the 93-94 season due to a debilitating knee injury.

Autographs are something that I never get used to—that people want my autograph because I play basketball. Playing basketball is something that I've been doing since I was a kid. To this day, though, it's a great feeling and an honor whenever someone asks me. It kind of means that you've arrived. The first time I signed was in college at Clemson. I had never thought about signing for someone before I was asked.

Curly Neal
HARLEM GLOBETROTTERS

One of the world's most famous basketball personalities, Curly Neal has been entertaining fans around the globe with his unique ball-handling mastery. Timeless in his appeal and ability, Curly is widely recognized as a true basketball legend.

I've signed autographs in elevators, bathrooms, pools, bull rings, every place imaginable. The Globetrotters brought me everywhere, and I've met great people around the world. Unforgettable people from Australia, Japan. Italy, England and Germany. I'm the luckiest guy I know, to have met so many wonderful people— and all because of basketball! With all of those beautiful smiling faces out there that you meet, there's nothing I want to do more than smile right back. Autographs and pictures are just a part of that.

Greg Norman
GOLF

The most exciting player in contemporary golf, "The Shark's" daring play around the globe has made him one of the world's most popular athletes. The winner of almost 60 tournaments worldwide, including two British Opens, Greg has earned more than $7,000,000 in competitive golf. The winner of two Vardon trophies and two Arnold Palmer trophies, Greg also hosts a tournament that bears his moniker, The Franklin Funds Shark Shootout. A native of Australia, Greg is both a humble winner and a gracious loser, true qualities of a great and enduring champion.

I've been approached from virtually every angle imaginable, and in so many places that not one instance really stands out. What is surprising is that the most aggressive group of people is the elderly women. They're not shy at all about coming right up to you and commanding your attention.

Autographs are part of the job. Because of our work, we choose to be in the spotlight. Being with the public is something that you need to work at just like your golf game. People see you on TV, and they think that they know you. You come to them out of that little box, and because of the way you play and conduct yourself, your personality is on display. Every athlete's or actor's performance is definitely a form of personal expression, and the fans think that they know you personally because you've shown so much of yourself through your profession. I understand the mindset, because I know what it's like to first get to know someone through their professional demeanor, and then get to know them personally. When I first met Clint Eastwood at the AT&T, I sat down had a beer with him. It was like I had known him for years, because I had seen all of his films and admired his work for years. The bottom line is that you can't shy away from the public. You're there because of your abilities, so it's important to try and enjoy it.

Athletes and Autographs

Ken Norman
ATLANTA HAWKS

A former All-American at Illinois, Ken is the prototypical power forward. He is a tremendous rebounder and defender and can also score from the outside. A hard-working competitor, Ken brings rock solid stability (15 points and seven rebounds per game) to Lenny Wilkens' front line. Ken was selected in the first round by the LA Clippers and became that franchise's all-time leader in points scored and games played.

It amazes me that people want autographs. What do people do with all of them? Where do they go? Is there a big file called "autographs?" Most players think that it's a big business, especially the cards. We know that someone is making money off of the signatures, we just don't know exactly who. Is that little freckle-faced kid going to put the autograph into his own collection or give it to his daddy to sell? Everyone likes to sign for the fans, but I don't think anyone wants to be tricked into signing something that will be sold to those same fans elsewhere. I've never collected autographs, but it wasn't a big deal to my generation. I guess when you put a value on something, you automatically make it worth pursuing, and that's the world we live in. If I were going to ask for anyone's autograph, I'd ask both Julius Erving and Mike Tyson. I'd definitely want their autographs.

Jay Novacek
DALLAS COWBOYS

Troy Aikman's clutch target, Jay is one of the most dependable Cowboys. A graduate of Wyoming, Jay's toughness is a key component to the Cowboys' success. He lead all tight ends in receptions for 1992, and consistently comes up with the big play. A quiet leader, Jay is well-respected by his peers in the game and is consistently voted to play in the Pro Bowl.

A kid from Wisconsin once wrote me. Why he was a fan of mine, I do not know, but he wrote me a letter that I will never forget. It was obvious that he came from a tough background from what he wrote. He said; ".....people like you don't sign autographs for dumb little kids like me.......at least that's what my stupid Uncle says." So I got a big laugh, and when I wrote him back, I made sure to enclose two autographed pictures. One I addressed "To Johnny," (not the child's real name), and on the other one, I wrote: "To Johnny's Stupid Uncle." Johnny never wrote me back, but I did keep his letter. In fact, I even put it in my scrapbook.

Hakeem Olajuwon
HOUSTON ROCKETS

A principal member of "Phi Slamma Jamma" at the University of Houston, Hakeem was the first overall pick in the 1984 draft, two picks ahead of Michael Jordan. He instantly starred for the Rockets as one-half of the original "Twin Towers" with Ralph Sampson and has become the best player in franchise history. All-NBA five times, a nine time All-Star, and twice the league's Most Valuable Defensive Player, Hakeem was finally named the NBA's MVP for the 1993-1994 season— a long deserved honor. However, his greatest achievement is being a part of the Rockets' 1993-1994 Championship season.

Autographs are about humility. If kids look at me and are speechless because they like my game or recognize me from TV, I need to demonstrate that I'm a normal guy and that I enjoy meeting them as much as they seem to enjoy meeting me. It's an honor to spend a few seconds and sign something for them. I'm only a basketball player, an entertainer. I'm human, just a regular person, and I should treat people nicely. Just because I am lucky enough to be a basketball player doesn't mean that people should make more of me than is necessary. Surgeons are life-savers and should be recognized for their work. That's more important than basketball. Basketball should not be about idol worship. You only worship God. The most important thing I do is to let people know that I am human.

Sign Language

Leslie O'Neal
SAN DIEGO CHARGERS

The Chargers' hard charging defensive lineman from Oklahoma State, Leslie attracts a lot of attention from opponents trying to block him. Leslie is not only a great pass rusher, he defends the run very well. His efforts are by no means overlooked by his peers, as attested by his four trips to the Pro Bowl. Leslie holds the NFL mark for most sacks recorded by a rookie (12.5), and has amassed more than 80 career sacks.

I like to sign when I can and especially if it means something more than just a souvenir. I was once involved with the United Way where they were trying to help this guy in San Diego who was trying to raise seven kids, two with serious spinal disorders. It was a heart-breaking situation because the kids were all pulling together to try to make everything work out. I made some appearances and tried to help raise money so that he could take care of his family. So many people deserve a hand, and it's nice to be able to lend it.

Shaquille O'Neal
ORLANDO MAGIC

Twice the College Player of the Year, Shaq was the first pick in the 1992 draft. His immediate impact was known as his thunderous dunks and court savvy helped him score more than 23 points and clear over 13 boards per game. Shaq was also an overwhelming choice for Rookie of the Year and was the first rookie ever to be voted Player of the Week in his first week as an NBA player. He was also the first rookie since Michael Jordan to be voted to start in the All-Star game, and he demolished two backboards in his inaugural campaign. But Shaq improved in his second season, almost leading the league in scoring, finishing second to Utah's Karl Malone.

I sign autographs every day. I talk to school children, visit hospitals, and spend a lot of time with the public. The main thing is— if I'm not doing something, or going somewhere, I'll sign for almost anybody. But sometimes people don't understand. The other day I was at the Hard Rock Cafe and this lady came up to me and asked me for my autograph. I said, "I can't do it right now, ma'am, I'm leaving."

"Enjoy your millions." She said sarcastically. "Enjoy your millions. I just want one autograph."

"Miss," I said, "I can't sign autographs right now, I have to go home." We had just had a game, and I was tired. There were a lot of people there, and if I signed for her, I would have been there all night. Some people understand, some don't— that's society. I like to do things for kids, charity groups and the disadvantaged. But I won't do anything for anyone who is rude.

Athletes and Autographs

Sign Language

Arnold Palmer
GOLF

A great driver (as evidenced here by his big rig), Arnold is known as "The King" to many and is one of those rare athletes to have influenced millions of fans while dominating his sport. Arnie's personal and professional charisma inspired legions to form an army of loyal, appreciative fans that both play golf and follow his career. His trademark charges and aggressive play led him to 60 PGA victories, 10 Senior PGA victories and 19 international titles. He won eight major championships and has been inducted into the World Golf Hall of Fame. Arnie's name also adorns the annual trophy awarded to the tour's leading money winner. Most importantly, his example has transcended the game. Arnie is a champion who would help his amateur playing partner look for a lost ball, and for that quality, is a member of the Hall of Fame of life.

The good news is that someone sees you and they want your autograph. I don't think that I've been anywhere in the world the last few years where I haven't been recognized and asked for an autograph. People approach me on the golf course, on city streets, and even in my plane. We've opened up the emergency door many times to sign for someone on a runway. Travelling around, I've seen the popularity of autographs grow. Australia, Canada, England, Scotland and Japan are all places where collectors and fans want to meet you and get your signature on a program or visor. In the 60s, autographs were popular, certainly in golf circles, but nothing like now. My own office spends over $150,000 mailing autographed pictures and things to people who send requests.

Alan Page
NFL HALL OF FAME

An original member of the Vikings' "Purple People Eaters," Alan was one of the best defensive linemen of any era. An All-American in college and All-Pro as a professional, Alan dominated the line of scrimmage at every level of play. Alan ran marathons while playing football and studied law. He is now a circuit court judge in Minnesota. When discussing role models, people need to look no further than Alan Page, Esq.

In my day, it was only the kids that approached you, now everyone is getting into the hobby. I'm no longer affiliated with football, and in my job as a judge, I still get requests from people who remember me as a player. I always oblige the requests, I'm only amazed that they still ask. After all, I'm only a judge.

John Paxson
CHICAGO BULLS

A deadly outside shooter, John will undoubtedly be remembered by Chicago (and Phoenix) fans for his championship series-winning three-pointer. His last-second heroics (which caught nothing but net) gave the Bulls their third consecutive NBA title. A graduate of Notre Dame, John was an academic All-American. A great guy, John is one of the most popular players in the history of the Bulls franchise.

Early in my career, people always gave me my brother Jim's card to sign, but now that we've won some championships, people are putting my card in front of him. Turnabout sure is fair play.

When I was ten year's old, I got Artis Gilmore's autograph at a college All-Star game, and twelve years later, we were playing on the same team! I didn't keep it. But I remember him scribbling a big "A" and then a few scratches. I wish that I had kept it. It would have been fun to show Artis.

Gary Payton
SEATTLE SUPERSONICS

The second overall pick in the 1990 draft, Gary has emerged as the Sonics' team leader. He is a tenacious baseline-to-baseline defender and a career double figure scorer. An All-American at Oregon State University, Gary has become an All-Star in the NBA through hard work and court smarts.

I have a special fan in Seattle. A little girl who goes everywhere I go. She's an American Indian and makes me belt buckles and things. I've kind of adopted her as my god-daughter. She's about five years old and has a little brother and sister, and I just adore this girl. She has no fear to come up and give me a hug and kiss, and she knows how much I like her. Her whole family is going to invite me to visit their reservation. She has been queen for the past year and has to give it up, and I want to visit her while she still holds that honor. People always ask me about celebrities I know, and sometimes I tell them that I hang with royalty.

Sign Language

Chuck Person
SAN ANTONIO SPURS

A high-scoring sensation from Auburn, Chuck has been an NBA star since entering the professional circuit. Chuck, primarily a perimeter player, is one of the best offensive forwards in the game, averaging almost 18 points per game in his career. He is a torrid streak shooter but also an exceptional passer.

Autographs have become a big time industry for many people, but kids still get a kick out of getting them for a variety of reasons, so they'll ask whenever they get the opportunity. There is no question that it is important for us to sign for the kids. Because as a professional athlete, it is our responsibility to the public to perform that service. People talk about athletes as role models, but I'm not sure that is right. Parents should be role models, because athletes— hey, we're still kids ourselves and in need of going through the maturation process of life. But if a moment with a kid can provide a thrill and a positive feeling, it is a privilege to be a part of it.

Mike Powell
TRACK AND FIELD

With an incredible leap of 29 feet, 4 1/2 inches, Mike Powell shattered Bob Beamon's long-standing (23 years) world record in the long jump event. Mike's record jump in Tokyo gave him a victory in the 1991 World Championships and preceded his silver medal performance in the 1992 Summer Olympics. Mike's rivalry with fellow great Carl Lewis has thrilled fans for many years. Both competitors push each other to new heights.

During an hour autograph session in Europe (and I mean one hour to the minute), a fan had brought a picture for me to autograph but was still pretty far back in the line when the hour period was up. I saw him in the dispersing crowd trying to get the picture to me, but he was having no luck. I was whisked away from the scene by a security force who ushered me into a waiting car, and on to the high security hotel where we were staying. When I reached the hotel, I saw him, the guy from the signing session, running like mad toward the hotel doors with several security guards in hot pursuit. He was flying! He reached me within seconds and gave me the picture to autograph. As I finished signing and handed it back to my fan, the security team had him by both arms and were trying to drag him away. Hard won, and (I hope) worth it.

Mark Price
CLEVELAND CAVALIERS

A former star at Georgia Tech, Mark has blossomed into one of the league's best point guards. Mark is a multiple All-Star player, an All-NBA first team selection, and the winner of the three point shot contest in 1993. He was also a Dream Team II team member and the career NBA free throw percentage leader (.908). A second round pick by the Cavs, he is their all-time assist leader. Mark's game is characterized by hustle, quickness and clutch shooting. Off the court, Mark is a devoted family man who has recorded spiritual music.

You sign so many, and the ones that stand out are the ones that you know help people who are sick or disabled, because a little effort on your part means a lot to them. And it's nice to do something for someone who is in a less fortunate position. People do want you to sign different things. I've even had some people take off their shoes for me to sign.

Dave Rahn
SAN FRANCISCO 49ERS

A veteran public relations specialist, Dave has handled his media related duties with elan and impeccable judgement. Furthermore, his cordial and sanguine nature allows him to flawlessly execute the duties of his job and embolden the spirit of those around him.

One time this middle aged Marine walks up to Head Coach George Seifert in the locker room and says, "Mr. Walsh, can I have your autograph?" George laughs, looks away, shakes his head and says, "They still get me confused," to no one in particular. And George doesn't try to correct the Marine's mistake. Instead, he starts to sign his autograph while the Marine tells him, "Us Marines have all the respect in the world for you, Mister Walsh, and that's why I called you 'Mister.'" Meanwhile, Rickey Watters has been watching the whole thing, and he can't contain his laughter any longer. "Hey," he tells the guy, "You got the wrong guy. That's coach SEIFERT, not Walsh." And the Marine went away a little embarrassed, but with an autograph.

Ahmad Rashad
NBC

A former star wideout with the Vikings, Ahmad has become one of football's most popular commentators. A speedy and tough competitor as a player, Ahmad is one of NBC's brightest personalities as an announcer. Ahmad will forever be remembered for his on-air proposal to his wife, Phyllicia, delivered via Bob Costas from the NBC studio.

Someone once came up to me and asked me to sign Lynn Swann's autograph. I knew that I wasn't Lynn Swann, but it seemed like this guy really wanted Lynn's autograph. Being an accommodating guy, I gave him the autograph he wanted and signed Lynn's name.

Andre Reed
BUFFALO BILLS

Jim Kelly's favorite target, Andre is one of the league's best all-around receivers. He has the speed, strength, concentration and smarts to consistently beat his opponent. He has caught passes for more than a thousand yards in a season three times and been a Pro Bowl selection five times. Andre is the Bills' career leader in receptions (586) and yards (8,233), and he holds the team record for most catches in a game (13).

My policy is to give back the attention that is given to me. If I get stopped in public, I'll sign if I have the time. I also respond to my mail, and I get lots of that. Bags and bags are there from fans all over the place. Even though it piles up, I make sure to sign for every request I get. If someone has the interest to send me something, I can respond, but it does take time, and I'm a player first. The bottom line is that if someone is that much of a fan, and they really want my autograph, I'll sign somehow, somewhere.

Sign Language

Athletes and Autographs 129

Mary Lou Retton
GYMNASTICS

Mary Lou bounded out of West Virginia and into the hearts of the world as America's first gold medal gymnast in the 1984 Los Angeles Olymipic Games. A spunky, energetic acrobat, she also became the first female athlete to adorn the cover of a Wheaties cereal box. Mary Lou now resides in Houston and still maintains a high profile in the world of gymnastics and Olympic sports.

I've signed for people of all ages, especially a lot of Wheaties boxes— not too many Energizer packages, though. Two strange items that I recall successfully signing were a banana peel and a diaper— that was used!

Andre Rison
ATLANTA FALCONS

Andre is the Falcons' record holder for receptions, yards and touchdowns in a single season, and is on a pace to hold every other significant Falcon record. An All-Pro selection and frequent visitor to the Pro Bowl, Andre is one of the strongest and toughest receivers in the history of the game.

There was this enormous pile of kids begging me for my autograph. I couldn't believe the size of the swarm, and at the bottom, there was this one little guy who couldn't have been more than four years old. I could barely see him, but I felt sorry for him because he was being squished by the other kids. So I reached down, scooped him up, and gave him my autograph. About 20 minutes later, he came back to me and asked for another signature. I looked down at him, and I just knew that he was up to something. So I asked him, "Little fella, who are you working for?" He then put his head down, to act ashamed, and he told me that it was for his dad. I smiled and signed for him again. I could tell that he was a smart little kid.

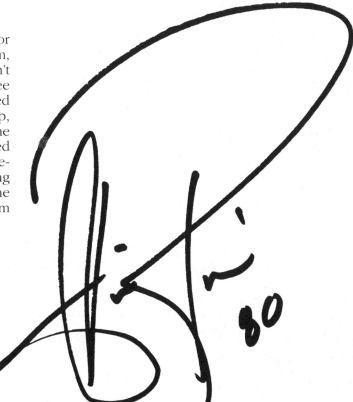

132   *Sign Language*

Cal Ripken Jr.
BALTIMORE ORIOLES

Cal has been a standout player from the moment he first stepped out on to the Memorial Stadium grass. Rookie of the Year in 1982, Cal has since won two MVP awards (1983, 1991), set 10 fielding records and the record for most home runs by an AL shortstop. At 6'4", Cal is the tallest starting shortstop in MLB history and an annual All-Star selection. Cal's legacy to the game will undoubtedly be his pursuit of Lou Gehrig's consecutive games streak of 2,130 games. Currently over 2,000, Cal is on a pace to eclipse the Iron Horse in 1995.

The most important autograph that I signed was to my wife, and I didn't even give it to her directly. I met her mom first when she recognized me in public and asked for an autograph for her daughter. She gave me the old line, "Have I got a daughter for you." At the time, I was single, so I was hearing that a bit, and I didn't think anything of it. She told me that her daughter's name was Kelly, so I signed the autograph by writing, "To Kelly, if you look anything like your mom, I'm sorry I missed you...." A few weeks later, I was making an appearance, and this girl comes up to me and says, "I understand that you met my mother..." And somehow I remembered that her name was Kelly. We started dating shortly thereafter, and, as they say, the rest is history.

Glenn "Doc" Rivers
NEW YORK KNICKS

A graduate of Marquette, Doc has been one of the most consistent and prolific point guards in the NBA. An injury sidelined him for the 1993-94 campaign, but he looks forward to coming back to help the Knicks get over that last hurdle on their championship quest. Doc also spends a considerable amount of time speaking to youth groups.

After this one game with Atlanta, I can't remember where—I'll say Indiana, it was cold and stormy and we had to fly to New Jersey. There was a huge storm there as well. It was cold, snow flurries everywhere— just miserable weather, and it delayed our plane. We finally landed about 3:00 AM, and when we got there, there was this one guy, about 19 years old, who was waiting to get our autographs. His only problem was that he had to wait outside in the snow and cold, because they wouldn't let him wait at the gate. So this poor guy had been standing in the wind and the cold for hours just waiting for us to arrive. All in the hopes of getting our autographs! Anyway, Moses Malone, who never signs autographs, takes one look at this guy and says, "Hey, I don't sign autographs, but any man that waits in this— I'll sign for him." This inspired the whole team, so we all ended up signing for him.

Cliff Robinson
PORTLAND TRAILBLAZERS

Cliff is a mobile, athletic and emotional star who ignites the Portland team when he comes off the bench. A great shot blocker and scorer, Cliff was voted the league's best sixth man in 1992-1993 when he averaged over 19 points per game, and became the Blazers' go-to guy in clutch moments. Cliff is famous for his rotating head bands, red, black and white, which reflect his on-court disposition.

Nothing extraordinary has happened to me. People are always pretty friendly and courteous when they recognize me. I sign for the fans as long as I am not in the middle of something, because I know it's fun for them. Like most people, I like to see the kids, because it's so obvious that they're excited to meet you. One time a little kid asked me if I had a special headband just for signing autographs, and that made me laugh. I told him that I didn't, but it wasn't a bad idea.

Jeremy Roenick
CHICAGO BLACKHAWKS

The flashiest star on one of the NHL's best teams, Jeremy is one of the top goal scorers in the league. His intuitive feel for the puck and quick bursts of speed have enabled him to be one of the youngest players in league history to score 50 goals in a season. An All-Star and fan favorite, Jeremy is a native of Boston, and a very good golfer.

I had just paid my toll in the automatic lane on the tollway and one of the guys that supervises the express lanes saw me reach out to pay and started to chase me down the highway as I was pulling away. He was running between cars, dodging traffic and waving his arms to stop me. I saw him in the mirror and stopped to see what was wrong. When he got to the car, he was out of breath, but asked me for my autograph. By this time, we were well away from the toll booth, but I signed and drove away. I figured that he recognized my license plates. They say JSR 27.

One Tough (and Smart) Customer

When I was ten years old, my father took me to see the Golden State Warriors play the Seattle SuperSonics. I recognized Seattle's coach as the guy in the AT&T commercial that had a basketball hoop in his office and could make a no-look, one-handed shot over his head. My Dad recognized the coach as Bill Russell, basketball legend.

Dad told me a little about Russell's greatness, and suggested that I ask him for an autograph. Looking back, Dad probably only wanted to catch a few moments of peace and quiet to enjoy his hot dog. Little did he know that I was about to learn an enduring lesson from an NBA great.

I had never asked for an autograph before and wasn't really sure of the procedure, but I do remember the moment. The reflection of the arena lights made me squint as I walked up to the Sonics bench. By the time I stood next to coach Russell, I had to angle my neck to 45 degrees just to see him.

"Mr. Russell," I started, "ummm, could I have your autograph?" Nervousness set in somewhere between the 'Mr.' and the 'ummm.'

"Son," the legend asked me, "what's the value of another man's signature on a simple piece of paper?" Before I could reply, he smiled, patted me on the head and said, "Sorry, I don't sign autographs," and walked away. His logic confused me, and by the time I made it back to Dad, I had learned that basketball players are both tall and clever.

I later found out that Russell did indeed go to great lengths to avoid giving his signature. A friend, Art, once wrote him a check in exchange for a promotional speech. Art knew that Russell did not sign autographs, but felt confident that he would at least get to see the former Celtic's signature on the check endorsement line.

Russell, however, did not cooperate. He could outsmart his opponents both on the court, and on the autograph beat. Instead of signing his name, the Hall-of-Famer wrote three words on the reverse side of the payment slip: "For Deposit Only."

Mark Rypien
CLEVELAND BROWNS

Born in Calgary, Alberta, Mark moved to Spokane, WA and became a high school legend there before attending Washington State. Mark was a sixth round draft choice by the Redskins and eventually became their starting quarterback. He led them to a victory in Super Bowl XXVI and was named the game's MVP. An aggressive, down-field thrower, Mark threw for almost 16,000 yards and over 100 touchdowns in his career with the Skins. Mark signed with the Browns in 1994 to bolster their quarterback position. A great golfer, he won the CGA tournament in Edgewood, Lake Tahoe and is notorious for his links prowess.

My brother's wife is a teacher, and she knew a boy that was paralyzed in a car wreck. He was a good athlete, and that was taken away from him in one quick moment. Meeting him certainly brought my perspective into focus. When I think about the challenges that face him and thousands of others just like him, it makes worrying about football seem insignificant.

In terms of being in the public eye, I know that people look up to athletes, and I try to make myself accessible so that people can see that I'm a normal guy. I imagine that it's tough for someone like Michael Jordan to get that balance between his public and private life. But it's something that I've been able to do—and I enjoy both parts.

Sign Language

Rony Seikaly
GOLDEN STATE WARRIORS

A consistent double-double performer in points and rebounds, Rony is still developing into one of the league's best centers. He has been the Heat's man in the middle since being drafted with the 9th pick in the 1988 draft. He was traded to the Warriors at the beginning of the '94-95 season.

In Miami, my little cousin once asked Moses Malone for his autograph. Moses brushed him off without signing, and my cousin came crying to me that Moses didn't sign. I said, "Hey listen, sometimes I do the same thing." But that experience made me think that an autograph can mean a lot to little kids and that there are times when you brush them off not knowing that they are going to be really hurt. This makes me think that I should be courteous and not take my position as an athlete for granted when I'm around kids.

Barry Sanders (signature)

Sign Language

Barry Sanders
DETROIT LIONS

The 1988 Heisman Trophy winner from Oklahoma State, Barry has been an NFL star ever since the ink dried on his contract. His inimitable style of directional change, cutting, and bursts of speed and strength have made him one of the league's best runners. After five Pro Bowl seasons, Barry is the team's all-time leading rusher with almost 7,000 yards and the leader in touchdowns scored (65). The 1989 Rookie of the Year, Barry has averaged almost five yards per carry in his career. All-Pro, All-Madden and All-Everything, Barry is a superstar whose talents awe fans and fellow players alike.

Over the years, the one thing that I've come to realize is that autographs can mean a lot of different things to different people. As an athlete, you sign so many that it becomes easy to forget what you're signing for people and why they want it. Adults, children, friends and family members all ask for autographs. Some want to keep them for themselves, others want to give them away as presents, and some want to donate them as charitable auction items. My basic philosophy is that I like to sign for good people at an appropriate time. That keeps everything short, sweet and simple.

Brian Shaw
ORLANDO MAGIC

The NBA record holder for most three-point field goals in a game (10), Brian is one of the league's most versatile guards. Brian, an efficient ball handler and passer, can handle the duties of both point guard and shooting guard. As graduate of UC Santa Barbara, Brian was originally drafted by the Celtics where he starred before going to Italy to play for a year. He teamed with Danny Ferry to star in the Italian league, eat pasta and enjoy the Roman ruins before being lured back to the NBA.

Someone wrote me in Santa Barbara and asked for my help with a school project. The student was a high schooler, and he wanted to just ask a few questions, so I wrote back and told him that I would help him. He was from Boston, and it turned out that the Celtics drafted me and his parents were season ticket holders in one of the front rows. We all got to know each other and became friends. The guy ended up going to the University of Arizona and became an agent. He doesn't represent me, but we are still in touch with each other.

Clyde Simmons
PHOENIX CARDINALS

Originally a ninth round draft choice by the Eagles out of Western Carolina, Clyde became a Pro Bowl performer for Buddy Ryan's Eagles. He led the NFL in sacks (19) in 1992 and resigned with his mentor following the 1993 season. Clyde brings his 76 career sacks and deep respect for coach Ryan to the Valley of the Sun and their campaign to qualify for postseason play.

When I was a kid growing up, I knew this family from my hometown. They had a son as well, who I had met once. Years later, when I got to Philadelphia, I was walking down the street, and a policeman walks up to me in his uniform and asks for an autograph. It was the guy from my hometown. Seeing him in Philly reminded me that it can be a small world, and that no matter where you are, you are never far from home. And, it was nice to know that I had a friend on the police force.

Mike Singletary
CHICAGO BEARS

One of the most accomplished linebackers in the history of the NFL, Mike is also one of the greatest gentleman to have played any sport. Mike, who was elected to 10 consecutive Pro Bowls, was the spiritual and physical leader of the famed "46 Defense," perhaps the greatest defense ever assembled. The leader of the Bears' Super Bowl XX championship team, Mike's intensity and ability always inspired his teammates. Having retired at the close of the 1992 season, Mike will surely be inducted into the Hall of Fame on the first ballot.

Both in Chicago and in my hometown, people don't approach me that often. In Chicago, I'm rarely out. And in my hometown, I was rather introverted growing up and did not get around at all. But I don't mind people approaching me, because they are usually very nice about it. I like to go to hospitals and schools, because the people you visit appreciate your presence. But it's apparent that autographs are a big business today. It blows my mind to see what the memorabilia is worth. I like it when charities and deserving groups benefit from autographed items, but they aren't the ones that normally do. It would be best to ensure that the business part of autographs benefitted deserving groups.

Sign Language

Scott Skiles
WASHINGTON BULLETS

A former star at Michigan State, Scott has made his mark in the NBA as one of the league's most tireless, relentless and effective point guards. He has even set the single game record for assists (30). Traded by the Magic to Washington, Scott comes to the nation's capital to bring his ball-handling wizardry to the young and talented Bullets.

I was playing for Orlando, and we were in New Jersey when this guy came up to me with a basketball under his arm. He looks at me and says, "Scotty, Scotty Skiles— you're great. I'm a big fan of yours. I've been following you since Michigan State. I love the way you play, you're a tremendous competitor. You're going to have a great, long NBA career...," and he went on and on. The he goes on, "I've got this sports bar down the street, and I was wondering, uhhhh, if you could get Shaq to sign this ball for me." I laughed and told him that he would have to get Shaq's autograph himself.

Emmitt Smith
DALLAS COWBOYS

One of only a handful of backs ever to lead the league in rushing three consecutive seasons, Emmitt is the focal point of the Cowboys' ball control offense. He holds club records for most yards (1,713) and touchdowns (19) in a season, and he showed the courage of ten men by playing with a separated shoulder in the '93 playoffs to lead the Cowboys to their second straight Super Bowl. Emmitt, appropriately, was the MVP of Super Bowl XXVIII and was lucky enough to celebrate at Disney World.

The Dallas Make A Wish Foundation contacted me and told me that a child wanted to meet me. He was very sick and a big Cowboys fan. It humbled me to think that one of his last wishes was simply to meet me. I know that in a long and healthy life, you get to wish for many things. When you're sick, your wishes are limited.

We were supposed to meet at a predetermined place one morning, and he didn't show up. We then made plans to meet at a local Ronald McDonald house that afternoon. Again, he didn't show up. Finally, we made plans to meet at my radio talk show that evening. At last he came, and we had a great time laughing together. I autographed some things for him and made a point to introduce him to the studio audience. They gave him a standing ovation. It was hard not to be moved if you saw the emotion in the room. I'll never forget that day, and I don't think that anyone who was there will be able to forget either.

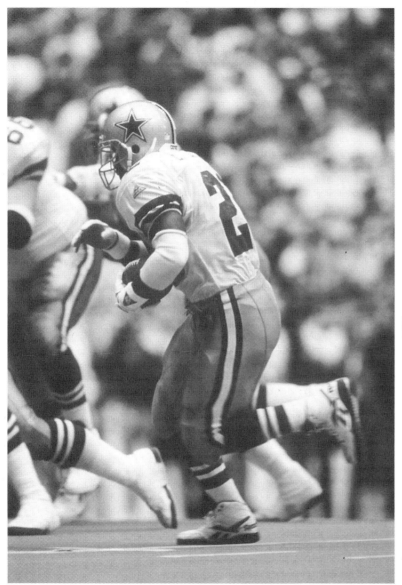

Athletes and Autographs

Charles Smith
NEW YORK KNICKS

A major factor in the Knicks' assault on an NBA title, Charles is one of coach Pat Riley's indispensable big men. Originally drafted by the Sixers with the third pick in the '88 draft, Charles was immediately traded to the Clippers where he became a star player. He has averaged 16 points and seven rebounds a game in his NBA career.

I was a Junior in high school and went to another town to watch a friend play in a tournament at the Jewish Community Center. At halftime, I was walking near the court when I heard a person—and I'm certain that it was an adult— say to his child, "Hey, you ought to get that guys' autograph. It's going to be worth something someday." And he was talking about me! I couldn't believe it, but it made me feel good at the time. So this little kid came up to me and asked me for my autograph, and that attracted about five other little guys. And that was my first autograph session.

Lee Smith
BALTIMORE ORIOLES

Baseball's all-time saves leader, Lee has been one of the best closers that baseball has seen. Primarily a power pitcher, Big Lee can also work the plate and change speeds to get the job done. He has a career ERA under 3.00 and has averaged almost one strikeout per inning pitched. With more than 400 saves and counting, Lee is a certain inductee in the Hall of Fame.

When people see me in my uniform, they sometimes think that I'm Lonnie Smith, because of the "L. Smith" on the back of my uniform. Or when I'm out of my uniform, they think that I'm either a basketball or football player because of my size. When I tell them that I'm a baseball player, they look at me funny and say, "baseball?" as if it's a big surprise to them. One day I'm going to tell someone that I'm a golfer.

My hero growing up was Dr. J. He was everything. Still is. Anyway, I was buying shoes a few years ago in a sporting goods store in Philly and I saw him in there. I got excited and bought a basketball right then and there. I walked up to him, introduced myself, and asked him to sign it. He was very nice, and the experience reminded me of how I felt before I was a professional athlete. It also showed that there's a part of me that will always be a fan.

Sign Language

Ozzie Smith
ST. LOUIS CARDINALS

One of the greatest shortstops ever, "The Wizard" is certainly one of the best players of his era. Ozzie has practically averaged a Gold Glove award per year (14/16), and he is one of the most consistent and exciting players ever to lace up the spikes. A switch hitter with more than 2,300 hits, Ozzie is tied with Honus Wagner for having at least 20 stolen bases for 16 consecutive seasons, a baseball record. Originally a San Diego Padre, Ozzie has become an institution in St. Louis. Famous for his trademark flips to start the season, Ozzie also owns a great bar/restaurant that bears his name in Westport Plaza, St. Louis. Lastly, Ozzie is also the first athlete of that great city to be named "Man of the Year."

Kids will ask you for an autograph, and I like to tease them, "So who is your favorite player?" "Willie McGee," they always seem to say. They always name someone else, and it makes me laugh every time. I think every kid tells each player that he's their favorite athlete in order to get an autograph. We might not admit it, but we all like to hear it.

The toughest autographs are the ones that you give in the hospital. Deep down, you know that some of the faces that you see are not going to live. They will not walk out of the building like I will be able to do. That makes me think about who I am, and that I'm lucky to play a game for a living. So when I walk into a room of a sick person and see them smile, I'm thankful that I can do that small thing for them. It gives me a rush to add something positive to another's day.

Rick Sutcliffe
ST. LOUIS CARDINALS

Rick is only one of six pitchers to have won 50 games in both leagues. He was the NL Rookie of the Year in 1979, that league's Cy Young award winner in 1984 and the 1992 AL Comeback Player of the Year. He started the first game ever played at Camden Yards and won by throwing a shut-out. Perhaps most importantly, Rick won the prestigious Roberto Clemente award in 1987 for his humanitarian efforts in the community. Now a Cardinal, Rick is a Hall-of-Famer on and off the field.

In 1989 I went to the Children's Memorial hospital in Chicago, and I met this one little boy who had leukemia. When I walked into his room, I had some t-shirts and things and I saw his Mom at his side. The boy wouldn't even look at me, and the mother was almost rude. It was like she didn't even want me there. She said, "Set the things over there and go on."

I asked them, "Would you like me to sign a baseball?"

She replied, "We don't want you to sign anything."

That rejection made me feel that I wasn't doing something right, and that I was bragging by going in there to sign an autograph— like that gesture would take away someone's pain. When I walked out of his room, I stopped and thought that maybe what I was doing was wrong. Maybe I wasn't being helpful by going to visit just because I as a ballplayer. I really felt that I had made a mistake by going in that room, and I didn't know what to do. Should I go on? Should I go home? I was confused as to what to do next. Finally, I continued on and gave away all of the things that I had.

About a week later, I received a letter from the boy's mother, and the writing was smeared all over the page because she had been crying as she wrote it. She wanted to say that she was sorry for her actions, and that after I had left the room, her son turned to her and said, "Mom, I'm glad that I have leukemia." At that, she started crying and asked her son what he meant. "Do you know who that was?" her son asked. "That's Rick Sutcliffe, and if I didn't have leukemia, he never would have come and visited me." (She hadn't known that I was a baseball player).

After reading that, I started to cry, and I couldn't help but be caught up in the emotion of the moment. It solidified what a guy told me a long time ago from the Big Brothers and Sisters program in Cleveland. He told me that 10 minutes of my time was worth more than 10,000 of my dollars, and I have never forgotten that. If I ever needed proof of that, it was in that letter that the boy's mother sent me. I've still got the letter, and I'll never forget what it stands for. From then on, no matter how awkward I feel, or how difficult it can be to see someone in pain or emotional distress, I always try to remember the lesson of that one boy and his mom. Maybe one moment can help somebody.

When I now visit a child, I give them my home phone number, and tell them to call me when they get well. I'll get them tickets to any game they want to attend. The program is called the IOU program, and I buy 50 tickets to each game to make sure that I can accommodate every request. This helps me break the ice with the kids, and it hopefully gives them something to look forward to during their recovery. The tickets aren't a cure, but it gives the kids something to get excited about.

Athletes and Autographs

Susan St. James
SPORTS FAN EXTRAORDINAIRE

Most people know Susan as the famous actress from series like MacMillan and Wife *and* Kate and Allie, *but she is also an enthusiastic sports fan. Married to NBC Sports chief, Dick Ebersol, Susan has had the opportunity/privilege to attend many sporting events and witness the excitement, hysteria and humor of sports entertainment first hand. A good sport, Susan has an excellent autograph memory that any celebrity could appreciate.*

I was at a big, pre-event party, maybe a Super Bowl reception, and someone came up to me and asked for an autograph. Before I could sign, he said, "I know who you are."

"That's nice," I said and smiled, "I'm Susan St. James."

"No," he insisted, "no you're not."

"Yes, I really am Susan St. James."

"No, you're not, definitely not," he repeated.

At this point we were arguing like a couple of children. "So," I asked him, "Do you still want my autograph?"

"Not if you think that you're Susan St. James," he said, and walked away disgusted.

Steve Tasker
BUFFALO BILLS

A special teams demon from Northwestern, Steve has made his mark on the NFL and been a major contributor to the Bills' success of the early 90s. Steve is consistently recognized by his peers with Pro Bowl selections and was the game's MVP in 1993, when his blocked kick was returned for the touchdown that eventually led to the AFC's victory.

I'm the guy of permanent mistaken identity. People will walk up to me and ask, "Who are you?" Or they think that I'm Mark Kelso, a defensive back on our team. "Hey Mark, great game, could you sign this ball for me."

"No," I correct them. "I'm not Mark Kelso. I'm Steve Tasker, and I also play for the Bills." Then they act embarrassed, and eventually ask for my autograph. I sign for anyone who asks. It's another part of being a football player in America, and it gives me a chance to see who is rooting for us.

Chris Thomas
TRACK & FIELD

A wind running specialist from Southern California, Thomas has been a tenacious competitor in the middle and long distance events that he has entered. The UC San Diego mile record holder, winner of the 1984 Lake Tahoe High Mountain Challenge, 1987 Swedish Grand Prix "B" mile and, most recently, the 1994 Los Angeles Canine-Human Road Race, Thomas has since retired to a life of academics and civic duty. Known simply as "Mel" in many circles, Thomas continues to influence runners in his international travels.

I'm not sure how many autographs I've signed. All that I know is that the figure is much closer to three than 100. I was at this one event in Sweden, and I had not yet run in any races, and I looked pretty official with my spikes in hand as I walked to the track with some other runners. A bunch of kids swarmed us, thinking that we were star athletes. I gladly grabbed the paper from the kids and signed for them. They only wanted me to sign because I was foreign and could potentially be somebody. So to give myself some credibility and legitimacy, I signed each one, "Chris Thomas USA." I'm sure that the moment was much more special for me than those Swedish kids, and I was ready to aggressively sign other autographs, but I guess that was my one moment in the autograph sun.

U.S.A.

Derrick Thomas
KANSAS CITY CHIEFS

The prototypical linebacker, Derrick is the big play leader of the Chiefs' defense. He is consistently among league leaders in sacks, forced fumbles and tackles. Extremely fast, Derrick's instincts and smarts have helped make him football's best outside linebacker and a perennial Pro Bowl selection.

One Christmas, I went to a local hospital in Kansas City and gave away presents and stockings to the kids there. I met this one little boy who was very ill. I sat down with him, and we talked for a while. I gave him a stuffed animal and wished him a Merry Christmas. We ended up talking some more, and I found out that he had recently lost his mother in a tragic accident. I felt so sorry for him, and it hit me really hard, because no little boy should be without his mother. As we talked, he asked me what I wanted for Christmas. I told him that I only wanted to know what he wanted for Christmas, and he told me about this special race set. So I went out and got him the race set. But it turned out that somebody else had already got him the very same set. I then found out that he also wanted a stereo, and I went and got him that instead. It was hard to tell who was more excited when he got the gift, he or I. I'll never forget him.

Sign Language

Tom Tolbert
CHARLOTTE HORNETS

A former Warrior and Clipper, Tom has found an appreciative home for his bruising, tenacious talents in Orlando. Tom, a graduate of the University of Arizona, is a versatile forward who can score as well as defend other big men. Undoubtedly the most uniquely coiffed player in the NBA, Tom is as personable off the court as he is relentless on it.

I was in Indiana, and this kid runs up to me and yells, "Mr. Smits, Mr. Smits, Can I have your autograph? Huh, can I have it pleeaase...??" I looked at him and said, "Little kid, I 'm not 7'6"— and I don't run like I have disjointed knees.....I am not Rik Smits, and I'm not going to sign his name." That's probably the only autograph request that I've ever refused.

Trent Tucker
CHICAGO BULLS

One of the NBA's original long range bombers, Trent's three-point specialty made him one of the most prized players on his teams. Originally a Knick, Trent haunted his former team as a key member on the Bulls' championship teams. He holds the Bulls team record for most three-pointers in a game for sinking six straight.

I've been in basketball a long time and seen a lot of things, but nothing unusual has ever happened to me in terms of an autograph request. Even in New York, which is a crazy place, nothing crazy came my way.

Playing for the Bulls, though, allowed me to see the phenomenon of Michael Jordan. He is large— huge. I played with Patrick Ewing in New York, and he is a star— a big star. But Michael is larger than life, the star of stars. Everybody else is a distant second. Everybody. The amazing thing is that after watching him from afar, playing on another team, I thought that I understood his popularity. But playing with him revealed the unbelievable degree of his popularity and the way that millions gravitate toward him. For me, it's fun to see. I enjoy being around him and going out with him, because he handles the public so well, managing the stardom that he helped create. Playing on championship teams with Michael Jordan brought notoriety to all of us. Fans wanted to be a part of the Chicago Bulls. By approaching us for an autograph, picture or handshake, they became, in a small way, a part of us.

Bob Uecker
MR. BASEBALL

A former catcher with the Braves, Cardinals and Phillies, Bob "Mr. Baseball" Uecker has achieved notoriety as an actor, announcer and product endorser. Bob has appeared in the hit movies Major League and Major League II and also starred in the ABC sitcom, Mr. Belvedere. His memorable commercials for Miller Lite and Krylon paint have only added to his reputation as one of baseball's funniest personalities. A native of Milwaukee, Bob is the voice of the Brewers on WTMJ radio.

I was stopped in traffic in Anaheim, and I heard this guy shouting my name. I didn't know where the voice was coming from, when all of a sudden this guy was climbing out of a sewer and coming towards me. You see a guy willing to climb out of the sewer to meet you, and you have to say "Hi" to that guy. He quit working in a manhole just to talk to me. It probably blacked out power in a part of the city, but he wanted to ask for my autograph. I'm just glad that he didn't ask me to lunch.....

One guy tried to climb the scaffolding in Milwaukee just above the broadcast booth, and security came and it was a huge melee— and all over an autograph. The guy was hanging 100 feet in the air trying to get an autograph, and he ended up getting thrown out of the ballpark. Had I known that, I would have signed for him and saved him all the trouble. But it's wrong for fans to go through all of that for an autograph.

Wes Unseld
WASHINGTON BULLETS

The greatest player in the history of the franchise, Wes was also the most popular. After leading the team to two NBA titles and winning a league MVP award, Wes coached the team in the 80s and 90s. He is commonly regarded as the best outlet passer in the history of the NBA.

I saw Julia Child checking into the Ritz-Carlton, and I asked her for an autograph. She said, "Ohhhhh, OK," in that famous voice and gave me her autograph before we both walked happily away from the encounter.

Sign Language

Kiki Vandeweghe
BASKETBALL

One of the NBA's most prolific scorers, Kiki had a tremendous career as a Clipper, Knick, Nugget and TrailBlazer. He was an All-Star multiple times during his tenure in the NBA as well as an All-American at UCLA. In his long NBA tour of duty, Kiki averaged over 20 points a game.

At my first All-Star game, I was walking down the podium, just excited to be a part of the event. I was getting everyone's signature and asked Bill Russell for his autograph. He refused to give it to me and was the only one not to sign. He is one guy that really won't sign autographs, and that is his prerogative. I sign for everyone, but I don't feel good about signing cards, because that's business for the recipient, not a fan memento—and I'm not sure if that is right.

Mo Vaughn
BOSTON RED SOX

The BoSox's best left-handed hitter, Mo is a rare power hitter who consistently hits for a high average. A rookie who showed great potential in 1992, Mo delivered big time in 1993 by leading his team in home runs, RBI's and total bases while almost batting .300. He followed that up by leading the Red Sox again in virtually every important hitting category in 1994. An active community leader, Mo devotes a significant amount of time to civic issues and is one of Boston's most popular and revered athletes.

My very first baseball card came out when I was playing in the Cape Cod League, and people wanted me to sign it. It wasn't my first autograph request, I started receiving those in college (Seton Hall), but it made me feel like an official, professional player. It's funny to me, because I always played baseball for the game, because I loved to play— nothing more. Not because I wanted fame, or to be treated like a celebrity. I don't collect autographs, but I do ask for other players' bats. I have Jack Clark's, Cecil Fielder's and a few others.

Loy Vaught
LOS ANGELES CLIPPERS

Loy embodies the qualities needed to succeed as an NBA big man. A natural power forward, Loy also has the versatility to play center and the other forward position. A contemplative, scholarly individual off the court, Loy is one of the best read players in the NBA.

There was this girl— a school teacher, who was apparently a big fan of mine and wanted to meet me. She may have even had a little crush on me. She was very shy and couldn't really ask for an autograph for herself, so her friend kind of pushed her in front of me. As I was signing something for her, I tried to make a little conversation with her— the ol', "Hi, how are you doing? What's your name?" That sort of thing— and I noticed that she wasn't really responding. I looked at her for a moment, noticed that she was trembling and she said, "Oh my God, this is incredible," as if meeting me was important. I felt a bit strange, because she was about my age. I never expected to see somebody be so emotional about an autograph, but she was.

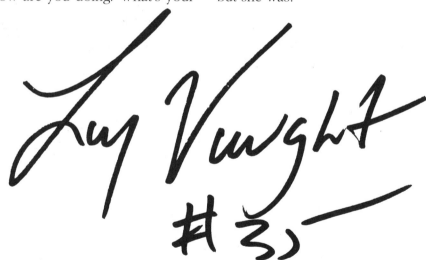

Frank Viola
BOSTON RED SOX

The 1988 Cy Young award winner with the Twins, Frank finished 24-7 (2.64 ERA) during that memorable season. Frank has also been one of baseball's best left-handers for the past decade, having won in double figures every year. He was the 1987 World Series MVP, and he has won 20 games in both leagues (Twins & Mets). A native of the East coast, Frank went to St. Johns before beginning his All-Star major league career.

When I warm up before a game, I usually concentrate so much that I focus only on the game and nothing else. I block everything around me out. Once in Cleveland, though, I was warming up and noticed a boy in a wheelchair. He was watching me, and something about him struck me and captured my attention. I finished my warmups, found a pen, signed the ball and handed it to the boy. Usually I just flip it to the pitching coach, but not this time. He gave me a big smile. He wasn't expecting the ball, but glad to have it. For me, it was a pretty special moment.

Chris Webber
GOLDEN STATE WARRIORS

One of the "Fab Five" from the University of Michigan, Chris Webber has been a standout player and fan favorite around the country at both the collegiate and professional levels. A two-time All-American at Michigan, Chris led the Wolverines to two straight NCAA title games before turning professional in 1993. He was the first pick in the NBA draft by the Orlando Magic, but was immediately traded to the Warriors. He became Rookie of the year after averaging over 16 points a game, and wowing NBA fans with his charismatic play. Chris is quickly establishing himself as one of the premier passers in the league, and teams with Latrell Sprewell, Tim Hardaway, and Chris Mullin to form one of the most exciting teams in the NBA.

One of the funniest fans that I've come in contact with was a student from Indiana University. She had real long hair down to the middle of her back, and she told me that she would shave her head bald if we beat Kentucky and got to the finals. We kept teasing her, "You're going to have to cut your hair. You're going to be bald once we win." "I'll do it," she said, "if you beat Kentucky." We weren't supposed to beat them, but after we won, we were looking for her. Sure enough, she was bald. She hadn't cut her hair for a few years, but she sure did after that basketball game.

Sign Language

Rickey Watters
SAN FRANCISCO 49ERS

A second round draft choice from Notre Dame, Rickey broke his foot in his first year with the 49ers, but made up for lost time by quickly establishing himself as one of the league's best backs. A relentless cutting, spinning runner, Rickey rushed for more than 100 yards in his first game, and over 1,000 yards that season and was voted to play in the Pro Bowl. He established the single game mark for touchdowns scored in a playoff game (five) against the NY Giants, and again made the Pro Bowl his second year in the league. His one goal now is to help the NFL's most potent offense get to the Super Bowl in the very near future.

At Notre Dame, I visited this child in the hospital who was in a complete body cast. This poor little guy could only lie down, watch TV and play Nintendo. I hung out with him for a while and tried to make him laugh. It's tough to see kids like that. It really messes with your mind because the kids are so helpless. You feel so sorry for them, and you can only hope that you made them feel a little bit better by being there and signing an autograph. Maybe when they look at it later, it will motivate them to get healthy themselves. Stuff like that makes me feel lucky. I know that health is a gift.

Lorenzo White
HOUSTON OILERS

An All-American at Michigan State, Lorenzo became a star with the Oilers, averaging over four yards per carry his first six seasons with the club. The 1992 season was Lorenzo's best season, as he gained over 1,200 yards, caught 57 passes and won a berth in the Pro Bowl. After fighting back from a serious injury in 1993, Lorenzo returned to Jack Pardee's Oiler attack in 1994.

I was in Alabama at a hospital which specialized in treating cancer patients. The ward was full of people in various stages of health, and it was obvious that some of the patients only had a short time to live. I made a point to visit each room, sign something and stay as long as I was welcome. The harsh reality of the situation was enough to make anyone cry. It was so sad. By seeing and talking to the patients, I was touched by their struggle to fight for life. They all hold a special place in my heart.

Reggie White
GREEN BAY PACKERS

Dubbed the "Minister of Defense" for his prowess on the football field and his status as a practicing minister off the field, Reggie White is arguably the best defensive lineman in the history of the NFL. Reggie is not only the only player to have more sacks than games played, but he is also a seven-time Pro Bowl participant and a former NFC Defensive Player of the Year. A longtime Philadelphia Eagle, Reggie signed with the Packers in 1993 and hopes to lead them to a Super Bowl. Reggie will soon pass the great Lawrence Taylor for the all-time sack leader distinction on his way to Canton, Ohio and the Pro Football Hall of Fame.

I've signed a lot of autographs in my career and taken many pictures as well. I've even been asked to dinner several times, but it's usually for that very night, so there is never really a chance to give a rain check. The only thing that I don't like is when girls want to hug me, especially if Mrs. White is around. Other than that, I'll gladly sign for anyone at anytime. However, there is one exception. I will not sign any autographs in the church. As a minster, I do not want the attention on Reggie White the football player, I want the attention on Christ and His teachings. Church is a sacred place, and I let the congregation know that I won't sign there. But if they can catch me on the street, I'm all their's.

Gerald Wilkins
CLEVELAND CAVALIERS

Gerald joined the Cavs in 1992 after starring with the Knicks for seven years. A career double figures scorer who excels in the open court, He is also a tireless defender. The younger brother of Dominique, Gerald is part of one of the best brother combinations in the history of the NBA.

I was getting my hair cut in this Cleveland barber shop and this little girl walked up to me out of nowhere and she went crazy. She was about eight or nine and very articulate. She said, "Hey, you're Gerald Wilkins." I told her, "That's right." She looked around at everybody in the shop and said, "Aren't you guys excited? This is Gerald Wilkins." She then said, "Don't go anywhere, I'll be right back. I've just got to have your autograph. I've got your card in the car, and I'll be right back." She then just sat down and stared at me— right after she told me that she'd be right back— and just stared and kept looking at me, unable to say anything. Everybody in the shop got a big kick out of her. She finally left and came back with her mom and a whole big stack of cards for me to sign. What a great little girl. Looking back on it, it was probably as great a thrill for me and the others in the barber shop as it was for her.

Sign Language

John "Hot Rod" Williams
CLEVELAND CAVALIERS

A product of Tulane University, where in the immortal words of Dave Shepard, "He lit it all the way up and down Bourbon Street." Hot Rod has since been one of the NBA's best sixth men. His scoring and shot-blocking seamlessly blend into the multifaceted Cavalier attack.

When I meet little kids, they always ask me two things: One, "Can I have your autograph?" Two, "How did you get your nickname?" I give them my autograph, a smile, and tell them that my stepmother gave me the name because I liked to scoot around as a baby.

Micheal Williams
MINNESOTA TIMBERWOLVES

A top point guard for many years, Micheal came to Minnesota from Indiana in the Pooh Richardson trade and immediately settled in as one of the leaders of the Timberwolves. Micheal is a consistent top ten finisher in both assists and steals, and he also set the league record for consecutively made free throws in 1994.

When I was with the Pacers, we were at this hotel when this older lady came up to me and said, "I heard that the Indiana Pacers were here." So I told her, "Yeah, there they go right over there," as I pointed down the hall. Since I'm only 6'2", I don't look like what people think of as a basketball player, so in that instance, I got away with not signing an autograph, but she chased down the rest of the team and made them sign for her. The guys got on me, but I told them that it was their fault for being 6'8" and 6'9" tall.

Another significant autograph experience happened when I was a rookie and I played against Maurice Cheeks for the first time. I had idolized him and Gus Williams growing up, but only Maurice was still in the league when I started playing. He was a great competitor and real classy off the court. So right before the game, I ran up to him and said, "I know that I have to play against you tonight, but I got to have your autograph. You're my favorite player of all time." When kids come up to me and tell me they admire me, I know what it feels like because I admired Maurice Cheeks in the same way.

Sign Language

Scotty Williams
PHILADELPHIA 76ERS

A key part of the Bulls' championship era, Scotty came to Philadelphia to bring the high effort, enthusiastic style of play that made him a popular and effective player with the Bulls. Scotty, who was a North Carolina Tar Heel as a collegian, hopes to bring his winning legacy to the venerable 76er franchise.

One time at North Carolina, this lady sent in a blue Tar Heel diaper for all of the players to sign. We all signed it, but I remember thinking that it might be sent from a North Carolina State fan— for her child to soil it. I hope that wasn't the case, because we all signed it, but you never know with that rivalry between North Carolina and State. People can get pretty clever when they want that psychological edge.

Walt Williams
SACRAMENTO KINGS

The seventh pick in the 1992 draft, Walt has been a dynamic scorer ever since he put on a Kings jersey, averaging 17 points per game as a rookie. An injury impeded his progress his sophomore season, but Walt's quick hands and excellent first step are a key to Sacramento's future success. A second team All-American his last year at Maryland, he set the single season scoring record of 26.8 points per game.

I was in Houston, standing outside the hotel waiting for a taxi when this lady came up to me and asked for an autograph. I said sure. "But," she said, "I want you to sign my butt!" And then she turned around, mooned me and ran away. Obviously she didn't get my autograph, but we both got a big laugh out of her prank.

Sign Language

Dave Winfield
MINNESOTA TWINS

Dave's career is distinguished by consistency, longevity and most importantly, productivity. One of only eight players to have 400 home runs and 3,000 hits, Dave is also one of the few players to have more than 100 RBI's with three different teams. The only athlete to have also been drafted by the NBA (Hawks) and NFL (Vikings), Dave's accomplishments in his chosen vocation will ultimately land him in baseball's land of immortality, the Hall of Fame. It should also be noted that his deeds off the field with his charitable organization, The Winfield Foundation, have won him the hearts of many more needy and deserving fans.

I was with San Diego and had only been in the big leagues a short while when this gentleman and his son walked up to me and asked for my autograph, and they were white. The father told me that he wanted his son to grow up to be just like me. Right then, I knew that baseball players held a special place in peoples' minds and hearts, and that it was a privilege to be a big league baseball player. All that mattered to the father was that I had worked hard and made the necessary sacrifices to achieve something— and I guess he wanted his son to have that same determination. So I learned at a young age that people look up to you. As a baseball player, people see how you act, and they want to emulate that. Learning that early in my career made me realize how lucky I was to be able to influence others and that it was an awesome responsibility to be aware of.

Orlando Woolridge
BASKETBALL

A high-flying, higher-scoring machine from Notre Dame, Orlando has been a consistent ingredient of "instant offense" for all of his teams, including the Bucks, Bulls, Clippers, Lakers, Nets, Nuggets and Pistons. A shot-blocking, explosive presence, Orlando's durability and competitiveness are the qualities that have endured throughout his career.

In Chicago this lady came up to me and asked for my autograph. I said, "OK," and she reached into her purse to grab something for me to sign. Without really looking, she just pulled out a bra and handed it to me. She didn't act very embarrassed, but I know that I was. She wasn't being fresh, she just didn't have anything else for me to sign.

Eric Wright
SAN FRANCISCO 49ERS

The best cover cornerback of the 1980s, Eric— along with Ronnie Lott, Joe Montana and Mike Wilson— is one of the four players who played on all four 49er championship teams. He also played in two Pro Bowls and made the most acrobatic interception in Super Bowl history against the Dolphins in Super Bowl XIX. A graduate of Missouri, Eric returned there to coach after having been a staff member with the Niners. A great player and person, he left his indelible mark on the game and the people he met along the way.

At training camp in Rocklin, these two pretty girls were sitting on the fence watching practice one day. They distracted me just by being there and caught my eye. One girl had on a pair of ripped jeans, which was the style at the time, and I couldn't stop looking at her. I was like a buzzard flying overhead, waiting to swoop down. I had a security guard bring them by after practice.

When I met them, they asked me for an autograph, and I knew that this was my opportunity to embarrass the one in the jeans. I signed a picture for the one girl, and I told the other girl that the only place where I could sign was where she didn't have a rip in her pants. She blushed and got laughed at by her friend. I signed her pants and walked away listening to her getting teased by the other girl.

Kristi Yamaguchi
FIGURE SKATING

Kristi burst into prominence by winning the 1991 World Championships in Munich. She followed that by winning the 1992 gold medal in Albertville in her graceful, athletic style. Kristi was one of five U.S. gold medal winners that year and has been a popular spokesperson for skating ever since. A native of Northern California, Kristi still devotes a lot of time to skating and its events.

Skating fans are really nice and very receptive. Here in the states and abroad, whether in Europe or Japan, people are always friendly and enthusiastic when you meet them. I feel that it's important to be gracious to the fans who so obviously show their support for us. Besides, I think that an autograph is a good excuse to meet the fans and show how much I appreciate them. Because of skating, I've had the good fortune to meet some really interesting people.

Kathy Bates, who starred in the movie Misery, came up to me in Los Angeles and said, "I'm your number one fan," just like she did in the movie. I laughed and said, "No! Don't say that."

Sign Language

Sign Language

Steve Young
SAN FRANCISCO 49ERS

The NFL's leading passer for the past three years, Steve is also the second highest rated quarterback in the history of the game. His ability drives the relentless juggernaut known as the 49er offense to its place as the NFL's best. The league's MVP in 1992, Steve is also the only 49er ever to throw for more than 4,000 yards in a single season. He is a charismatic player whose inimitable style puts him in that rare 'human highlight film' category and one of the NFL's biggest stars. An off-season law student and charity minded benefactor, Steve plans to practice law after his career.

In 1984, I came to Honolulu to play in the Hula Bowl. A Hawaiian girl who was part of the welcoming committee came up to me and wanted me to sign a part of her grass skirt. She pulled a long palm leaf right off her skirt and handed it to me. I signed it and handed it right back to her without giving it a second thought. Nine years later at the Pro Bowl, the same girl came up to me and showed me the palm leaf that I had signed all of those years before. She said that she had followed my career from the USFL to Tampa Bay and with the 49ers. The leaf still looked pretty good, and my signature was still legible. That goes to show you that tropical air is good for just about everything— even autographs.

About the Author

Phil Schaaf is life-long sports fan who lives in the San Francisco Bay area. He had just finished reading Shakespeare's *Hamlet* when he had the idea for this book. Not wanting to suffer the same mental torment as the fabled Danish prince, Phil researched and wrote this book over an 18-month period.

He currently works for Pacific Sports Marketing as a consultant on both media and retail-driven promotions in Northern California. He has worked with such companies as Carl's Jr., Coca-Cola, Dole, Long's Drug Stores, MCI, Nabisco Foods Group, Reebok, Safeway and $ilverbar Productions and Marketing in a variety of sponsorship sales and execution applications.

Phil would like to thank his benefactors/advisors and publisher. A self-proclaimed "leisure machine" with a permanent case of golf fever, Phil encourages any desultory soul to embrace the lure of blind ambition and/or to work like they live:"hard."

Aloha!